PASSPORT TO HEAVEN'S
Angelic Messages

PASSPORT TO HEAVEN'S ANGELIC MESSAGES

A Hands-On Guide for Communicating with the Angels

TONI KLEIN, ACP

PASSPORT TO HEAVEN'S ANGELIC MESSAGES
A HANDS-ON GUIDE FOR COMMUNICATING WITH THE ANGELS

Copyright © 2016 Toni Klein, ACP.

All rights reserved. No part of this book may be used or reproduced by any means, graphic, electronic, or mechanical, including photocopying, recording, taping or by any information storage retrieval system without the written permission of the author except in the case of brief quotations embodied in critical articles and reviews.

iUniverse books may be ordered through booksellers or by contacting:

iUniverse
1663 Liberty Drive
Bloomington, IN 47403
www.iuniverse.com
844-349-9409

Because of the dynamic nature of the Internet, any web addresses or links contained in this book may have changed since publication and may no longer be valid. The views expressed in this work are solely those of the author and do not necessarily reflect the views of the publisher, and the publisher hereby disclaims any responsibility for them.

Any people depicted in stock imagery provided by Thinkstock are models, and such images are being used for illustrative purposes only.
Certain stock imagery © Thinkstock.

ISBN: 978-1-4917-8693-2 (sc)
ISBN: 978-1-4917-8694-9 (e)

Library of Congress Control Number: 2016900440

Print information available on the last page.

iUniverse rev. date: 11/28/2020

To my precious son, Ian, my beautiful earth
angel and passionate football player!

To my loving husband, John, who has the biggest
can-do attitude of anyone I have ever known!

Contents

Preface ix
Acknowledgments xi
Introduction xiii

Chapter 1   An Introduction to Angels 1
Chapter 2   The Four Clairs 4
Chapter 3   Cleansing Your Space and Yourself 9
Chapter 4   Staging Your Area 17
Chapter 5   Meditation 20
Chapter 6   To Forgive and Forget? 26
Chapter 7   Expressing Gratitude 33
Chapter 8   Twenty-Five Ways to Remain Positive, Balanced, and Receptive 36
Chapter 9   Setting Objectives and Goals in Order to Communicate with the Angels 47
Chapter 10 The Dos and Don'ts When Connecting with the Angels 51
Chapter 11 Easy Ways to Receive and Recognize Your Guidance 65
Chapter 12 Living Your Life with the Angels 75

Epilogue 77

Appendix 1 Angel Experiences 79
Appendix 2 The Hierarchy of Angels 85
Appendix 3 Who Are the Archangels and Angels? 89
Appendix 4 Archangel Modalities 95

References 97
Journal 99

Preface

Ever since I was young, I have received messages from the angelic realm. It started at a very early age, and I never questioned it. My mother and grandmother were spiritually inclined, and I grew up hearing mystical stories and wonderful experiences. Therefore, my connection to the spiritual realm always felt very natural to me. Today, I am an Angel Certified Practitioner (ACP), certified Fairyologist, and hold certifications in Reiki, mediumship, spirit guide coaching, and past-life healing as well as being trained in dream interpretation. I have also assisted the church in the role of a Christ Servant Minister and instituted a homebound visitation committee and service.

Years ago, the angels suggested I write a book. I was flattered by the prospect. My purpose was to explain to society on behalf of the angels that they do exist, have specific purposes, and speak to everyone. It is important for my audience to realize that angels impart goodness and wisdom to all of us, not just to me or to other angel intuitives. Yet it is vital that everyone maintain an open mind in order to be receptive.

I sincerely thank my angels for their guidance as well as for placing me in contact with extremely special people who have been great help in my quest. The angels will bring certain individuals into your life to support you. In turn, one day you will most likely help someone else when he or she needs aid. It may not be the same being; it could be another who needs your particular help. It is a special feeling and produces good karma. The angels loudly applaud this kind of work.

First, I suggest reading *Passport to Heaven's Angelic Messages* from cover to cover. Next, reread chapters 2 through 11 slowly, and then follow the guidelines. Your results will not be instantaneous; however, it will be an enjoyable journey and learning experience. The pace for each person will vary. A journal is located at the back of the book. Please take notes, and journal your thoughts, your experiences, and all messages as they are presented to you.

Since I am a Christian, I will refer to the Creator as God throughout *Passport to Heaven's Angelic Messages*. However, please insert the name of your higher power if you follow another religious tradition.

My desire is to instruct you on how to be receptive while keeping you enthused and motivated as you read *Passport to Heaven's Angelic Messages.*

Enjoy the process!

Acknowledgments

I would like to share my thanks with the following earth angels in my life:

My mother, Rowena, and brother, Gustav, who have offered their support on this project.

Mimi, my spiritual doggie, the healer who loves being a part of my angel work.

Anthony J., who has been with me on this entire journey and who has been an absolute source of inspiration and encouragement.

My friend, Chuck, the "guru".

Hilda, my lovely "angel sister".

To those special people who have contributed their very personal angel experiences: Anthony J., Hank, Hilda, Jamie, Joan, and Rose Q.

To God and the angels, guides, archangels, and saints, whom I rely on every day!

Introduction

Welcome to the beautiful world of heavenly angels. It is my world and your world. Angels are among us, waiting for our call. They are direct energy sources from God sent to us for support and celestial care.

Passport to Heaven's Angelic Messages was endorsed by the angels and written in an effort to demonstrate how to connect to the angelic realm. They even helped me to create its title. I was given some leeway; however, the word *passport* was to remain. Today this special guide exists to assist anyone to connect, from the novice to the seasoned spiritualist. When this guide is followed correctly, the reader will receive and communicate with the heavens while attaining a high spiritual frequency.

In my experience, I have found that people receive in the range of fifty heavenly communications daily. Many individuals do not recognize them or simply do not pay attention, because of a hectic lifestyle, distraction, or lack of faith. I must convey that everyone has the ability to hear the messages from the Creator's heavenly beings. Yes, you too!

Passport to Heaven's Angelic Messages is designed to teach you how to open the channel of communication between you and the Divine. This handbook primes the reader not only to take the necessary steps to ensure proper communication but also to reach and maintain spiritual fitness. This may act as your preparatory guide to understanding the mission of the angels while developing and fine-tuning your skills. You will learn to use techniques that will optimize your abilities and sustain them, thereby allowing you to live a positive and soulful life. I offer ways to connect and receive heavenly communication successfully. You will learn to take the needed steps to hear, see, know, and feel messages. One must be a willing participant and do the work involved. Some days may be easier than others. It depends on the factors going on in a person's daily life. However, with purpose and belief, any individual may become proficient and attuned to the Divine.

In the following chapters, you will learn about the various types of angels and their different earthly purposes. In addition, treat *Passport to Heaven's Angelic Messages* as your preparatory guide to understanding the mission of the angels while developing and fine-tuning your skills. You will learn to use techniques that will optimize your abilities and sustain them, thereby allowing you to live a positive and soulful life.

Chapter 1
An Introduction to Angels

> Angels transcend every religion, every philosophy, every creed. In fact, angels have no religion as we know it … their exitence precedes every religious system that has existed on Earth.
>
> —St. Thomas Aquinas

Throughout the ages, humankind has been mystified by the angelic realm. For example, Michelangelo depicted angels in his legendary Sistine Chapel ceiling. Angels were also a popular subject for Byzantine and European paintings and sculpture. In modern times, angels also have a great deal of recognition and respect. Today, many angel collectibles, statues, and artworks are readily available to the angel lover.

The good news continues. A poll by CBS News (2011) reported nearly eight out of ten Americans believe in angels. Moreover, according to Duin (2008), half of the American population are angel believers. Mary Fairchild (2011), a Christianity expert, found the NIV Bible made reference to angels 273 times.

What is an Angel?
The primary definition of an angel according to Merriam-Webster: "an·gel noun \'ān-jəl\: A spiritual being superior to humans in power and intelligence; especially: one in the lowest rank in the celestial hierarchy."

We have often heard of angels referred to as messengers of God. In the Greek language, *angelos* means messenger.

What Role Do Angels Play?
Angels are sources of light and energy sent from God. The plan for these holy beings is not only to act as God's servants but also to serve as helpers and ministers to His creation. In God's kingdom, a hierarchy of angels is present. Various levels exist, and each has a unique assignment from God. The higher-level angels act as agents in the organization of God's kingdom. The lower levels (closer to earth) are assigned to act on behalf of humanity, minister to the needy, and guide us in the understanding of God's plan for salvation while protecting us from physical and spiritual enemies. More detail is listed in regards the hierarchy of angels in appendix 3.

According to the NIV Bible, just a few roles angels perform for God include the following:

- Messengers.
- Holy warriors.
- Praising and worshiping God.
- Guardian angels.
- Protecting and guiding mortals on behalf of God.

An angel may be present anywhere and at any time, when you least expect it. An angel may be the stranger you are speaking with in the grocery store who allowed you to go ahead of him or her in line. An angel could be a wisp of wind that blows by you on a hot summer day that leaves you feeling content and happy or the faint song you hear as the wind whistles though the autumn leaves. Don't assume angels will appear in an obvious way. Angels are pieces of the Creator, and they are around you each and every day. It is prudent to remain aware.

Remember—you never know with whom you are speaking throughout the day. The mysterious man who had asked you for the time may just have been an angel.

As the old adage goes, "With God, all things are possible."

> Be not forgetful to entertain strangers, for thereby some have entertained angels unawares. (Hebrews 13:2 NIV)

Chapter 2
The Four Clairs

So in a voice, so in a shapeless flame, angels affect us.

—John Donne

Angels communicate with us in four predominant ways:

- A very strong feeling, yet you have no supporting evidence that the information you were given is real. However you are confident the data is true because you "just know."
- A message resounds in your head in the form of a strong thought. Perhaps you hear a statement in an audible voice.
- A clear vision enters your mind providing important information. It appears as a quick flash, yet offers details.
- A powerful feeling overcomes you regarding a certain situation or person.

The scenarios described above are referred to as the four clairs. The spiritual community recognizes these clairs as the four categories in which an individual receives guidance in message form. The clairs include the following:

- Claircognizance (knowing).
- Clairaudience (hearing).
- Clairvoyance (seeing).
- Clairsentience (sensing and feeling).

1. Claircognizance

This refers to "clear knowing." An individual who experiences claircognizance recognizes in his or her core that the message received is absolutely real. The person will have an understanding of the information even though none existed prior to the person receiving it.

Illustration: Sarah had been introduced to an older man during a business conference. Sarah explained that as Paul was shaking her hand, she instantly knew they would eventually marry each other. At the same moment, Sarah received information Paul was seeking a religious pursuit, and she was to help him once they were married. All of this information was delivered to her in a few split seconds. *That's crazy!* she thought. Since Sarah's current relationship was complicated, she dismissed this information. A few years later, Sarah and Paul were married. Shortly after their nuptials, Paul became the pastor of a small hometown church as his second career. Sarah feels on that very day of the conference, so many years ago, angels were bringing her good news from heaven, and it was magical!

2. Clairaudience

This denotes "clear hearing." There are two variations of clairaudience. One is to hear thoughts clearly inside your head, usually in one's own voice. The second is to hear an audible voice outside of the body, just as if someone is speaking. These messages are meant for you, and only you will hear them. The messages are either pleasant or bring warning. Since communication is delivered from heaven, it is never malicious in any way.

Illustration: When I was a child, I lived on a farm. Our yard was surrounded by beautiful old oak trees. I enjoyed taking strolls around the farm, and my cats and their kittens would often follow me. One windy afternoon as I approached the line of oak trees, I heard a voice (outside of my head) clearly shout, "Watch out!" (It is important to note that no other human being was accompanying me.) I peered upward, and a huge branch was flying toward me. I dodged it just in time! "Thank you," I replied. My concern immediately turned to my little kittens and mother cats, but they were already gone. I do believe they received their own warning.

3. Clairvoyance

This means "clear seeing." This type of communication refers to being presented with images, movie-type scenarios, colors, pictures, or snippets of a scene in your mind's eye. Clairvoyance may be experienced with your eyes opened or closed. These appearances are your messages, and no one else can see them.

Illustration: I was in a new city for a convention a few years ago. As I was leaving my hotel room to walk downtown, I had a very quick vision of a man close to me on my left side. He proceeded to grab my handbag. This was all I received, and I saw it in approximately three seconds of time, but that was all I needed. Since it was necessary for me to go downtown and I could not find a taxi, I secured my bag and started out of the hotel. I was acutely aware of my surroundings more than ever due to this vision. As I walked, I continually checked behind me. After five minutes, I spied a man through the corner of my eye very close to me on the left side of my body. I turned quickly and shocked him. He was practically touching my arm but fled when he saw the look in my eye. If I hadn't been alerted by my angels through my vision, I surely would have been very unassuming and minus one handbag that day. Or worse!

4. Clairsentience

This refers to "clear feeling." To experience clairsentience means to sense a person's aura, vibration, energy, and/or feelings. Often, the individual will experience a particular gut feeling about a person or situation.

Illustration: Years ago, I was interested in building a new house on the property my parents had given to me. Therefore, I immediately scheduled an appointment to speak with a local builder and was very excited. I asked my father, Joe, to accompany me. The following week we met the builder on my vacant lot. After we all walked the property and had a discussion, I was enthused. I had felt everything was in line with what I was seeking price-wise and time-wise, and the builder seemed friendly. When the builder left, I eagerly asked my father his thoughts. He laughed and informed me I was foolish to employ this man to build the house. Disappointed, I questioned his reasoning. My father explained he received a very negative feeling from the builder. Furthermore, he cautioned me if I selected him, it would turn into a nightmare. He added he had no hard evidence to back up his feeling, but he was certain it was true. Can you guess the outcome? I did not listen to his angelic guidance and exerted free will. Free will is the choice to make our own decisions, whether they are good for us or not. I rejected his guidance and decided to hire that construction company. It proved to be the nightmare my father and his angels tried to tell me it would become. There were delays and other negative occurrences. That particular builder was not for me.

In life, sometimes we are so focused on what we desire we unintentionally block or ignore our own messages or those given to us by others, just as I had done. Therefore, if a trusted person in your world obtains important information on your behalf, as my father had done for me, please take it into consideration. Weigh your options, and don't ignore anything.

Habitually, we will experience one clair over the others as our strongest. After reading the four types, you may have already identified which one is your prominent clair. In most cases, the dominant clair will lead, and a secondary will assist it. In the case of the builder example, my father experienced a knowingness (claircognizance) in regard to the contractor being unreliable, which was coupled with a brief vision (clairvoyance) in which the new construction would experience delays, etc.

I have experienced having one particular primary clair guide me at one point in my life with the other clairs assisting. However, as time passed, my primary clair (hearing) switched to one that had been a secondary clair (seeing). I questioned why this had happened since I was happy with the way I received my communication. My contemporaries and angels informed me this is done by design. In order to become more proficient with the other clairs, it is necessary to switch up occasionally. In the event this scenario happens to you, don't feel you are losing your primary clair. You are just developing another!

Certainly, you will enjoy and experience all the clairs through sight, sound, thoughts, and feelings. It is truly a delight. Once recognized, the clairs will aid you in your daily life.

Tips:

- Trust your messages. You receive them for a reason.
- If the message given to you is unclear, ask for clarification immediately. Do not wait.
- When seeking affirmation, ask the angels to repeat the message. It is a good sign to receive a message more than once. In fact, if the same message is delivered to you three times, rest assured it is meant for you!
- Only good and productive guidance will be given to you since it is delivered from heaven.

Messages sent from the Divine are gifts, so stay tuned. These angelic beings are even more excited to communicate with us than we realize. How wonderful!

Angels have no philosophy but love.

—Terri Guillemets

Chapter 3

CLEANSING YOUR SPACE AND YOURSELF

Crying is cleansing. There's a reason for tears, happiness or sadness.

—Dionne Warwick

Spiritual cleansing is a vital effort for each of us. Cleansing may take place in a variety of ways:

- Cleansing of the mind, spirit, and body.
- Cleansing of a personal residence, work space, car, or any area you feel a buildup of negativity has taken place.

Unfortunately, it is a natural occurrence that negative energy will build up because of illness, bad news, arguments, ghost activity, or a streak of bad luck. This may result in what I call a drag in energy. We should make our space and ourselves as clean as possible in order to be clear receptacles.

My recommendation is to carry out periodic cleansings. My dwelling receives a cleansing once per month. However, you should conduct one without hesitation if your residence begins to feel heaviness in the air. In the event of a new home purchase, it is especially important to cleanse the old energy from it prior to your relocating.

Listed below are eight effective and inexpensive ways to rid negative energy. Once you follow these tips, positive energy will flow into your life. Your messages will not have to penetrate any negative build-up, and therefore will reach you clearly.

1. The Use of Salt

Salt is a natural substance used to rid negativity. Sea salt, not table salt, is suggested for the cleansing process. It is a wonderful and accepted resource.

To clear negative energy in the home, either place a teaspoon of sea salt or a mixture of salt and water in a small bowl or place it in each corner of the house. I suggest if you are utilizing the water method to change the water each day.

Another technique to get rid of negativity is to sprinkle sea salt only in the affected areas in your residence. For example, you may have an argument with your significant other in the family room or an unfriendly visitor in the foyer. When salt is drizzled in that particular area, the negativity will neutralize.

A sea salt bath will help dispel the negative energy from your body. First, light a white, unscented candle. Next, sprinkle sea salt into a warm bath. While soaking, focus only on positive intentions. When you are finished, dress in white pajamas or a white bathrobe. You may feel drowsy or sluggish, as if your energy has been momentarily exhausted. This is actually a very positive sign indicating the salt bath has worked. The depletion of energy signifies the bath has drawn the negativity from your body.

2. Ringing a Bell

Ringing a bell naturally removes bad energy while promoting a positive flow of energy. Historically, bells have been customary in places of religious worship and have a spiritual significance.

Last year I had the good fortune of buying a set of antique Sanctus church bells. I ring these bells when I feel the need to literally clear the air. Plus, I enjoy the melodic tone while performing the exercise. Any bell will suffice. Wind chimes are a useful device to get rid of negativity since they offer similar benefits as using a bell. I have multiple wind chimes on my property.

Ring a bell whenever you see fit.

3. Airing and Letting Light into an Area

Natural light is very beneficial to maintaining a positively charged space. As often as the weather allows, open the windows in your home and part the drapes. Try decorating a room with lighter, sheer curtains.

The use of direct sunlight for cleansing jewelry and crystals is beneficial. It can clear the energies attached to them. I place a new piece of jewelry or those I have worn on the windowsill to be cleansed. Through normal use, jewelry may accumulate negative energy. Consider this scenario: You have conducted interviews at your place of employment the entire day and have shaken many hands. As a consequence, you may have inadvertently been the receiver of another person's low energy. It is always best to cleanse jewelry after such a situation.

On the opposite end, the light of a full moon may be used to recharge crystals, rocks, jewelry, and other items.

4. Eliminating Clutter

Personally, I find this one to be difficult since I love buying meaningful things. Nevertheless, the mind flows better and messages are received much more easily in an uncluttered space. If the work and home environment are kept clutter-free, dusted, and as clean as possible, the mind will feel happier and unblocked. If you have a clutter tendency, as I sometimes do, leave at least one area or room free for meditation and guidance purposes.

5. Prayers

Protection and blessing prayers for the home are essential. You may request a family priest, pastor, Buddhist monk, or whomever you are comfortable with to visit and perform a blessing or cleansing ritual. My contemporaries and I have done this, and we highly support it.

A good friend, Rose, who practices Buddhism, kindly gave a Buddhist chanting box to me. It is one of my prized possessions. She suggested I select one of its many chant choices to play continuously in my home. Doing so will help to eliminate any residual negative energy and will bring additional blessings into the home. I was especially appreciative, since at that time, my husband and I owned a house that was built in the 1700s and was located in a triangle of cemeteries. One was located adjacent to our backyard, the second positioned a few houses down the road, and the third, on the other end of town. Occasionally, I had felt a spirit passing through. Although most souls seemed peaceful, an occasional spirit was not content. Therefore, I played the chant box in an effort to pray for any spirit passing through as well as to keep negativity at bay. The chant box is a helpful prayer facilitator as well as a meditation tool that keeps the positive energy flowing. It can be used in conjunction with Buddhist chanting rosary beads. Reciting the Catholic rosary or the Buddhist chant is a good means of protective prayer since the repetition creates a powerful mantra.

Archangel Michael is known as the angel of protection. He may be called on whenever you need an extra shield of safety. Today, whenever I walk through a cemetery, (one is located next to my current house as well), I pray to Archangel Michael for protection from any lower energies and to escort stray souls to the light.

6. Lighting White Candles

Lighting a white candle is a good way to elicit protection and purity. As I light my candle, I offer a prayer to Archangel Michael and ask that he surround my loved ones and me with his cloak of protection. Last year, I purchased an antique votive devotion candleholder that belonged to a church in the late 1800s. I enjoy lighting the candles and protecting my space while reveling in its beauty. There are plenty of interesting ways to decorate with candles and add protection at the same time.

As you extinguish the candle, be sure to use a candle snuffer or pinch the flame. It is not advisable to blow out the candle since it may be considered an act of disrespect to the element of fire. In ancient Greece, candles were placed on bread in an effort to pay homage to the goddess of the moon. Later, Germans placed a candle on a cake for religious purposes. Over the years, it evolved into the birthday candle tradition. Of course, to blow out one's own birthday candles is a happy tradition and safe to do. That's the exception to the rule in regard to blowing out candles.

7. Saging or Smudging

The premise behind burning sage, also referred to as smudging, means purifying with smoke. It is believed the smoke attaches itself to the negativity in the air, thereby releasing it and providing a spiritual cleansing. The negative energy is then transmuted into positive energy. The aim is to rid the negativity brought on by adverse situations whether it is in the home or another location. You may wave it around the body if negative energy is felt or as a safeguard.

A smudge stick is a combination of herbs that have been dried, placed together into a bundle, and tied together with string. It is recommended to always place the sage or smudge stick in a heat-protective holder. Special holders are sold for this purpose, or you may use a bowl or abalone shell as well. Supplies may be purchased online or in a New Age or spiritual store.

The following is my recommendation concerning smudging or saging:

- Prior to saging, open a window in every room, and utilize a fan. The goal is to force the smoke and negativity out of the residence.
- Light the sage or smudge stick. Burn for a few moments, and then snuff the flame. It will then burn like a lit cigarette.
- Begin and end the process at the front door.
- As the smoke fills the air, wave it around your body and cleanse yourself. Repeat at the close of the session.
- Enlist the aid of Archangel Michael, God, Jesus, or your Creator to assist with the cleansing work. I offer the following prayer to Archangel Michael as I enter each room: "Archangel Michael, please protect me during my cleansing process. Please lift away all negativity and send it to the light. Please replace with joy and happiness. Thank you." You also may create and recite your own cleansing prayer or walk in silence holding positive intentions.

- As you are walking through each area, slowly wave the smoke in a counterclockwise direction. In each room, cover as much area as possible until you reach the front door once again.
- After the cleansing has been completed, extinguish the stick by pressing it into a fireproof receptacle. Another option is to place the stick into a bowl of water that was prepared in advance.
- End the session by expressing thanks to Archangel Michael, the Creator, or the universe.

Caution: Guard against falling embers. Never leave the smudge stick or sage unattended. Always exercise caution when walking through the location to ensure burning embers do not fall to the ground.

The time you invest in performing cleansings is entirely your choice. I suggest conducting one whenever you feel negative vibes or heaviness in the air. The entire dwelling may be cleansed or just your sacred meditation area. Keep in mind, negativity naturally rebuilds itself due to adverse situations, such as an illness or a family drama. Therefore, the time between conducting cleansings may vary from person to person.

8. Cleansing Your Chakras:

What are the chakras? Phil Catalfo, in his National Health article in 2015, "Chakras 101," explains the chakra, or the wheel, is derived from the ancient Sanskrit language and made known by the yogic sages and pertain to seven energy centers of the body. It begins at the base of the body, runs along the spine area, and ends at the head. The chakras are known to embody an individual's physical, emotional, and spiritual makeup.

The seven centers are comprised of the following:

1. Root
2. Sacral
3. Solar plexus
4. Heart
5. Throat
6. Third eye
7. Crown

In order to cleanse all seven chakras or a specific one, various approaches are available. Choices include participating in a live class led by a seasoned instructor, purchasing a recommended book, online avenues, or through an audio source. When listening to a CD, please exercise caution, and never perform a cleansing while driving. This could prove dangerous since the process produces a very relaxed feeling and driving requires remaining highly alert at all times.

In general, chakra cleaning is a very worthwhile action anytime you feel clogged or messages are not being received as easily as usual. It also has other benefits, as in pinpointing an area that could use assistance. For instance, in the event an individual wants encouragement with communication skills, cleansing the fifth chakra, the throat chakra, is necessary. I support doing this in conjunction with asking Archangel Gabriel, the respected angel of communication, to assist. I endorse visualizing a clean throat chakra with light from heaven in conjunction with praying to Gabriel for strength and ease when communicating.

Cleansing the chakras ensures your vibration level will be at an optimum level and your messages may be received more easily.

9. Holy Water

Holy water represents water blessed by a priest, bishop, or person in an equal position. It can be used for rituals, blessings, spiritual cleansing, and protection against bad energy.

Personally, I like to keep holy water accessible in my house and handbag. I have been known to sprinkle a few drops on myself and my spiritual doggie, Mimi, for overall wellness. Each day we had a ritual. I called to Mimi and said, "Holy water, holy water." She would run over and wait for me to sprinkle it on her body. Periodically, I bless my house and car with the holy water. In the event I am about to walk into an unhealthy situation or have just left one, I place a few drops on myself.

I keep my holy water in a pretty, lightweight container I bought from a Catholic shop. Many Catholic churches offer fountains or receptacles from which to draw the water. Some churches have small bowls located in the front, while others have large, attractive fountains. The water is available free of charge to parishioners. You may wish to consider this an encouraging and inexpensive way to cleanse and feel protected.

10. Essential Oils

Essential oils have been in existence for many centuries. These oils have been used for spiritual wellness as well as a beauty aid.

Many oils are available for different arenas, including protection, prosperity, love, and success. These oils may be breathed in, dabbed on the skin, diffused, or placed into bathwater. Just a few drops will release its magic.

Below are two examples of the uses of essential oils and their special abilities:

- Frankincense: May be used before bedtime and is placed on the temples. It is said to produce a calm sleep and increase spiritual awareness.
- Lavender: Used to create a soothing environment and enhance relaxation.

There are various ways to spiritually cleanse. Remember to always ask your angels to help you. Be sure to get in the habit of speaking to them. They love to be by your side!

Sage is cleansing and sacred.

—Pink

Chapter 4
STAGING YOUR AREA

We all have angels guiding us … They look after us. They heal us, touch us, comfort us with invisible warm hands … What will bring their help? Asking. Giving thanks.

—Sophy Burnham

A fun and personally meaningful step to connect with the heavens is to spiritually stage your very own zone. Depending on the space available, you may decorate an entire room, a nightstand, a mantelpiece, a tabletop, a garden, an outdoor area, or anywhere you wish. This region should mirror your individual spiritual values and beliefs and no one else's. This sacred territory is a personal piece of art and serves as your private sanctuary. It serves as a comfortable refuge for you to meditate, pray, and connect privately.

The idea of a sacred personal place has gained much popularity as of late. Many individuals have designed their own area in order to reflect, pray, meditate, and communicate with Guidance. The spiritual valuables in your life adorn your environment. Some items may include crystals, angel cards, prayer cards, oils, God box, angel statuary, rosary beads, or anything else you wish. I have designated three spots in my living space. The first is my nightstand, which is filled with angel ornaments, prayer books, a journal, candles, crystals, and other special items. The second is a spare room which I have converted into a chapel. I selected my church votive candle holder and kneelers to be placed there. I enjoy lighting the candles in this old-fashioned piece as I seek particular answers. The third area is in the backyard. A portion of the lawn is devoted to a mediation garden. To adorn this special area, I selected a white wrought iron bench, an angel statuary, and a fountain.

Additionally, when staging your area, you may desire to apply the age-old Chinese principle of feng shui (pronunciation is "fung shway"). In a basic sense, to feng shui is to make a harmonious balance between your energy and your environment's energy. There are many believers in the use of feng shui. In fact in the United States, feng shui is a very popular and fertile business in the interior decorating world.

If you decide to design your special angel or mediation area using the art of feng shui, it is advisable to select a balance of objects with a mixture of shapes: circular, square, or triangular. Placement of the objects is key. For example, if items are placed in front of a window, it is best to use a sheer drape or a potted plant to reflect the energy back into the room. Additionally, if locating your angel altar in a corner that is dimly lit, add a source of light. This will act as a jump start for positive energy to flow. Another suggestion is to drape a piece of material on your altar table using red or deep blue colors. A good strategy is to identify one piece as your focal point since it captures your gaze. Adjust your look periodically by adding or deleting items in order to keep the energy fresh. Dust and spiritually cleanse the spot as necessary.

The altar or meditation room is your creative work of art and does not need to be set in stone. The pieces that adorn it may change or be added to, or the location may change. It's your choice. If you're unsure how to decorate, consult the angels!

Each day, at the same time, try to make an appointment with your angels to meet in your sacred space. Stick to this time frame. After having this period slated just for you and your angels, they will expect you at that time.

It is said these angelic beings are even more excited to communicate with us than we are with them.

Enjoy and connect!

> Her angel's face, As the great eye of heaven shined bright, And made sunshine in the shady place.
>
> —Edmund Spenser

Chapter 5

MEDITATION

If we know the divine art of concentration, if we know the divine art of meditation, if we know the divine art of contemplation, easily and consciously we can unite the inner world and the outer world.

—Sri Chinmoy

Meditation is essential in order to clear your channel properly and enhance your connection to the Creator, your Higher Self, and the angels. If conducted properly and with purpose, meditation enhances your channel and improves your health. Meditation, when done with intention, can be a monumental benefit to your daily life.

Meditation is known to foster mental relaxation and awareness. It can also help de-stress the physical body. I am certain you have heard people say to one another, "Take a deep breath and relax." There is much truth to that statement!

In the past, meditation had been thought of by some as only being conducted by monks in a land far, far away. According to *Yoga Journal* (2012), approximately 8.7 percent of US adults are practicing yoga. Moreover, many high-level corporate leaders have begun meditating for the health benefits it brings, as well as to gain a competitive advantage through discipline and other positive effects.

Mindfulness teacher Melissa O'Brien (2011), in her study "What are the cognition benefits of meditation?" reported by Quota.com, found many health benefits to meditation. A few include: the reduction of stress, which can lead to lower blood pressure and anxiety levels, increased problem solving, improved posture, heightened awareness, keener thinking, decreased levels of insomnia, and stronger leadership skills due to higher personal confidence levels and improved discipline.

Guess which celebrities practice styles of meditation? Some include Lady Gaga, Gwyneth Paltrow, Jerry Seinfeld, Howard Stern, and Oprah Winfrey, just to name a few.

Our goal is to focus. When we eliminate the distractions of our lives, the messages will come. Therefore, understandable and meaningful communication with your angels will be present. You will be mindful of the four clairs, and your dominant clair will prevail. A calm mind keeps the channel clear. Doesn't the car run better when it is cared for? We maintain our cars with oil changes, top offs, and detailing. Why not give ourselves the same attention?

Conventional wisdom recognizes two categories of meditation: passive and active.

Active Meditation
It is not the desire of everyone to sit still and perform meditation. Thankfully, for those who think the sound of it is dreadful, another type is available. It is known as active meditation.

When active meditation is conducted, the physical body is engaged in a repetitive activity. The mind is focusing intently on this particular event. By doing so, our consciousness is in a harmonious state for that moment in time. Therefore, meditation is occurring. Examples of active meditation are bike riding, swimming, washing dishes, folding laundry, reciting the Catholic rosary, or chanting.

Imagine the following illustration. One night after dinner, as your meditational session, you decide to wash the dishes. As you take a deep breath and clear your mind of all distractions, your focus is directed to the water pouring over the dish. You smooth the soapy sponge over the dish and rinse over one dish and then another. Your mind is only focused on the task and not allowing any outside thoughts to enter the mind. Pay attention to any messages that come to you. You have just conducted meditation. It is easier than you think.

Passive Meditation

Passive meditation is the act of quieting the mind by remaining still. There are many techniques to explore regarding passive meditation. Since over twenty styles of meditation exist, there are multiple choices! Listed below are a few in brief discussion. If one or more styles appeal to you, try them on for size and find a favorite.

Transcendental Meditation

Transcendental meditation, TM, is a mantra-style form of meditation popularized by Maharishi Mahesh Yogi. Yogi is better known as the guru to the celebrities, including the Beatles. TM became the rage in the 1960s through the early 1970s and is still widely practiced today. Over six million people in different age groups, cultures, and religious beliefs have learned TM. Various celebrities employ the transcendental method, including Clint Eastwood, Nicole Kidman, Madonna, Eva Mendes, and Katy Perry. I find TM to be one of the easier passive meditation methods.

In an interview with Charles Berger,[1] an angel intuitive with thirty-plus years of experience and wisdom, he provided insight into his personal experience with transcendental meditation.

Berger explained an individual who chooses to practice the transcendental method pays to receive his or her own personal mantra word in a workshop with TM personnel. For our purposes, he will substitute his private TM mantra word for the universal one, "Om."

First, Charles recommends the following: Choose a quiet area to meditate with no distractions. Next, sit in a chair, with your hands placed on your thighs, palms facing upward and your eyes closed. Then take four to five deep breaths in through your nose and out through the mouth. Repeat the mantra, "Om" aloud, and concentrate on stretching out the end of the

---

[1] From an interview I conducted in April 2015.

word. During the process, focus only on the mantra, and do not let outside diversions enter into your mind.

Berger's recommendation is to meditate five minutes per day as a starting point and to increase eventually to twenty minutes per day. He declares if your timetable permits, it is advisable to meditate at sunrise and sunset each day. The optimum is to conduct meditation twice daily if time allows.

Charles stated, "It's true while meditating, thoughts will flow into the mind. However, for meditation to be truly effective, we should remain in a state of nothingness. So, as the thoughts come into our head, we have to focus more on our mantra. When our minds are relaxed, thoughts and ideas will flow more easily. Essentially, we will make better decisions and lead a more stress-free existence."

Mr. Berger suggests this is the perfect meditation technique for the newcomer (as well as the more advanced individual) since it is easy to perform and a very practical method to fit around one's schedule.

Breathing Technique
The premise is to focus your attention only on your breath coming in and going out for twenty-minute intervals per day. The major component is to focus and remain in the current moment. It is not advisable to think about today, yesterday, or tomorrow but to concentrate just on breathing. This is said to build endurance and create a clearer mind-set, less stress, and a direct channel to guidance.

Heart Rhythm Meditation (HRM)
Heart rhythm meditation places attention on breathing and the heartbeat. During the HRM process, people seek to associate themselves with their hearts and become more in touch with their feelings felt from the heart. The participant is asked to take full, deep, rich, rhythmic, and balanced breaths. Once a person controls his or her breathing, it develops into becoming something more powerful, sensitive and compassionate in relation to the heart center.

Guided Visualization

Guided visualization is a well-known type of meditation and a good place to begin. It is practical for the person on the go. This is performed while following a live speaker or a prerecorded direction. It is usually conducted with the eyes closed in a comfortable position, and imagery is used throughout. Guided visualization does not originate from any rooted tradition. There are many CDs and YouTube videos available. This is one of my favorite types of meditation.

Trataka or Fixed Gazing

Trataka is a type of meditation practiced when the eyes are focused on one object: a candle, a dot, or another stationary object. By doing so, it is difficult for stray thoughts to enter into our minds. The rationale is if the eye movement stops, the mind will calm. Hence, the proper level of concentration has been developed. I do not suggest gazing for long periods of time on a candle's flame since it may not be healthy for the eyes.

Vipassana

A popular method, Vipassana refers to clear seeing, mindfulness, and being in the present moment. This technique is not about closing off one's thoughts but rather accepting all thoughts as they come. The key is to remain detached from these thoughts while remaining in the moment. It is said that a person practicing Vipassana does not change his or her breathing since it could alter the energy in the session to a lower frequency. As in all meditations, we are trying to raise our frequency and perform a spiritual self-cleanse. Vipassana is regarded as a popular method and stems from the Buddhist tradition.

Raja Yoga

Raja yoga, a form of yoga meditation, is termed the "path to enlightenment." It is said purification of the mind comes to those who practice it because residual negative karma from previous times is discharged. Typically Hindi or New Age music is played while the gaze is fixated on a picture of its founder or another image. This may be conducted by a trained teacher. The trainer will sit face-to-face typically eyes locked and meditate simultaneously with the study. The goal is to become one with the "Supreme Soul," therefore, leading to enlightenment on a larger scale. This meditation suggestion is for fifteen-minute intervals each day.

Zazen

Zazen, or "seated meditation," is said to be a more difficult version of meditation. It is conducted for extended durations and performed in a seated position (either on a chair or on the ground), sitting up straight with perfect posture.

There is no particular breathing style used. Originally created for the monk's style of living and environment, it is difficult to mimic in today's society.

The Internet, bookstores, and meditation class listings are fabulous ways to find more information and choose a technique for your lifestyle. With practice of the different styles available, you will be able to choose the one which is the right fit for your lifestyle and ideals.

Meditation done with intention will wash away the clutter and chatter in your daily life as well as create other advantageous results. No particular belief system is necessary—just a willingness to commit to the process and a receptiveness to connect and bring you closer to the spiritual world. Many people believe answers may only be found in the outside world. However, with the help of meditation, we can gain inner wisdom and answers from within and experience spiritual and personal growth. Our angel messages will then flow to us much more easily.

With meditation and remaining in the moment, it's a win-win!

~

> Sleep is the best meditation.
>
> —Dalai Lama

Chapter 6
TO FORGIVE AND FORGET?

Forgiveness is not always easy. At times, it feels more painful than the wound we suffered, to forgive the one that inflicted it. And yet, there is no peace without forgiveness.

—Marianne Williamson

Forgiveness—the ability to pardon another for a wrongdoing—is a healthy act and good for the soul. To offer another individual absolution is vital to one's spiritual well-being and is a positive choice to make in every way.

Oftentimes it is viewed as a form of vindication if one person does not forgive the other. Yet the unforgiving entity is only punishing him or herself. The overwhelming feeling of hatred and contempt will eventually consume the wounded person. The swirling of perpetual negative energy may even cause health problems later in life. In addition, one's spiritual frequency is at risk of being lowered, and this may trigger the inability to receive messages. This type of situation hinders the unforgiving and angered person in more ways than he or she realizes.

Meanwhile, let's concentrate on the offender for a moment. Yes, the person who caused the pain and angst. Most likely the following things are true:

a) He or she has already justified his or her actions.

b) He or she does not give the situation another thought.

c) He or she has moved on and may even be torturing another person at this point.

d) The offender is now holding power over the victim and has him or her in a mental hold.

This is a very vicious cycle. It may eventually lead to a form of mental imprisonment by not being able to let go of the situation. Is it really worth holding onto the hurt?

On the other hand, in some cases, the type of person does exist who truly desires to be forgiven for his or her wrongdoing. This individual deserves to be granted another chance. How would you feel if you hurt another and were truly sorry, only to be shunned by him or her?

In each instance, forgiveness as well as purging the memory of the event is key.

Why Forgive?

There is no single reason not to forgive. In fact, many health benefits are linked to the subject of forgiveness. The physical and mental paybacks are substantial. A few include the following:

- Lower blood pressure.
- Stronger immune system.
- Greater self-esteem.
- Less stress and anxiety.

The act of clemency is positive for everyone involved. Once a circumstance has been resolved, a lighter, happier heart as well as mental peace will be experienced. Granting mercy leads to an uncluttered and receptive mind.

Should We Forget?

An individual may say, "I have forgiven." However, the question beckons, "Should I or can I forget?"

Through my own research, I have established varying opinions do exist between men and women. In 2015, I conducted a poll that was divided equally between men and women, in the age range of thirty-five to fifty and in varying salary ranges.

The following question was posed to the participants: "If a person caused you hurt and anguish, which situation below would apply?"

a) I would forgive and forget all-inclusively.
b) I would extend forgiveness but never forget the event.
c) I would neither forgive nor forget.

The results of the forgiveness poll proved interesting. It demonstrated all men, with the exception of one, believed in forgiving and forgetting. To them, the occurrence was finished business. Meanwhile, only one-third of the female voters subscribed to forgiving and forgetting. The balance of women believed in forgiveness, yet they never wanted to forget the hurt caused.

Personally, I found the male viewpoint being so different from the women's regarding forgiveness very curious. Even though I'm guessing the male population does not realize it, it seems a man will not jeopardize his high spiritual frequency by being unforgiving.

Times When I Believe It Is Important Not to Forget

Yes, my opinion it is best to forgive and forget. Yet circumstances do occur that qualify as exceptions. For instance, a harmful situation may transpire, and it is vital to remember in order to remain on guard.

Illustration: When I was seventeen years old, my best friend and I often made plans together. She became very famous for breaking our engagements for a more attractive offer, which would arise always at the very last moment. I would then receive a phone call canceling our plans with no regard for my feelings. I was deeply hurt over and over. One day I decided this was not the type of friend I wanted in my life. I also decided to forgive her but to stay far away. It was important for me not to forget. I didn't wish to be lulled into making more plans and then crushed when it did not transpire. Although I forgave her transgressions, I made sure I did not forget and fall into the trap of letting it happen to me over and over. In this scenario, remembering offers a type of defense mechanism against future hurts.

Never compromise your healthy spiritual state by placing yourself voluntarily into an emotionally depleting situation. Ask the angels to place a pink light of love and peace around you and the individual in question. If you need to sever ties with the person, Archangel Michael may be enlisted. Request he cut the cords that bind you to a harmful person or event.

A prudent practice is not to perpetuate negative situations. Another case of to forgive but not forget relates to the individual who has been physically attacked. This person may choose to forgive the attacker yet not forget the event in an effort to remain aware.

A nonvoluntary situation in which negativity exists is not as easy to circumvent. Perhaps you are seated next to a coworker who is rude, bossy, and difficult. Since you are being paid to come to work, it would be unreasonable to walk out on the job. In order to manage this, you may try diffusing the situation. It could be as simple as mentally saying to the person, "I forgive the way you act toward me." Immediately after, send pink light and love to that person. Furthermore, enlist Archangel Michael to shield you spiritually from the mean-spirited one. In addition, invite a special team of harmony angels into the office to spread the feeling. I realize this is a difficult task. Yet it works and will soften the vibe in the room. You will reap the benefits of this undertaking, which will literally take a few moments. Repeat the process when necessary.

It is vital for our spiritual and physical health to forgive and in most cases, forget. It is important that you don't allow the offender to lord any power over you. Forgive. Don't torture yourself. It does not pay since all aspects of the body—physical, emotional, and spiritual—may be jeopardized.

Nevertheless, forgiveness is a personal choice since we are all human and possess free will.

Doreen Virtue shared a perfect quote in her book Healing with the Angels. She wrote, "Forgiveness does not mean, 'What you did is okay to me.' It simply means, 'I am no longer willing to carry around the pain in response to your actions." She continues, "Forgiveness releases you from the "prison" of another person's choices and actions and the effects they have on your life. When you are finally free, you can move forward to experience more peace, joy, and happiness."

I have given much thought to the subject of forgiveness after experiencing a few negative situations in my own life. After some self-reflection and analyzation, I developed ten tips on how to deal with forgiving and forgetting. They made me feel better. I would like to share them with you.

1. If you can't forget initially, it's okay. However, do forgive. I advise it is in your best interest, and you won't regret it. Move on, and leave it in the past. You cannot change what happened. We don't have a time machine—yet.

Ginger Alden, Elvis's fiancée, had written in her book, *Elvis and Ginger* that Elvis related his thoughts to her and said, "You've got to kill it and get it behind you. If something bothers you Ginger, you've got to kill it and get it behind you." He was referring to people who had hurt him in his life. I believe Elvis was right. His advice to "get it behind you" is a healthy strategy. Ginger, who was very young when Elvis imparted his wisdom to her, was fortunate to hear it early in her life. It impressed me, and I feel it is valuable advice for all of us. I enjoyed reading *Elvis* and *Ginger* and highly recommend it.

2. Unfortunately, the world does not stop spinning on its axis or take a day off for our particular problems. Do not dwell upon the hurt. It is a healthy stance for you to take. The best thing to do is to move on.

3. Realize it was not your fault. The other person betrayed or hurt you, not the other way around. It is his or her karma that must be dealt with, not yours.

4. Time is a healer. If the person was sorry and has not hurt you any further, the incident will fade. However, there will be times when further betrayals may take place. In the event you work with this person and do not have

the option to disassociate yourself, I suggest not engaging, remaining professional and aware, and moving past it.

5. Don't obsess about the event any longer. As the unhappy memory enters your mind, turn it around and think a pleasant thought ASAP. Most likely the people who have caused your hurt are having a pleasant day and have dismissed it. They are not reliving it each day, and neither should you. Replace the negative thoughts with positive ones immediately. Eventually with practice, the bad memory will fade away.

6. Ask yourself if anything positive came from the situation. I personally believe there is always a positive aspect in every negative situation if you look. For example, perhaps you were hurt yet learned not to be so unassuming in the future. Or possibly the person who betrayed you was a chain smoker who always lit a cigarette in your presence even though you were allergic to the smoke. Your health instantly improved since now he or she is absent from your life. There is always an upside. Trust me.

7. Focus on yourself. Take the time to do something fun. Rest and heal.

8. Release. To hold onto a negative circumstance may eventually affect your relationship with friends, your partner, or others. Initially most people demonstrate kindness and listen to your story. However, since it is not their story, eventually most will grow tired of listening. It is not kind but nevertheless true.

9. Break the chain that keeps you held to this situation or person through forgiveness. Whether you know it or not, you are bound to this person through nonforgiveness. Freedom is so important to all of us. An individual should never hold any power over any of us, especially because of whatever nasty thing he or she did! Certainly do not relinquish your personal power to anyone. It is surely not a healthy way to live.

10. Always speak to your angels and ask for their assistance. As you would seek solace with a close friend, have a heart-to-heart conversation with these celestial beings. They will not only help heal the situation, but it also will be to everyone's benefit. Oftentimes a solution will be presented that may never have occurred to you. When involving the angels in the process, you will feel healing benefits immediately.

Truth be told, if you were seeking forgiveness, wouldn't you want the person you hurt to cut you that break?

To forgive is golden and so very beneficial for you spiritually and physically. An important aspect to forgiveness is that the channel to communication will be open and clear. You will receive messages and goodness into your everyday life because you are relaxed and focused.

The next time you have the choice to forgive, remember all the benefits you may reap.

Always forgive your enemies; nothing annoys them so much.

—Oscar Wilde

Chapter 7
EXPRESSING GRATITUDE

> Be less of a complainer and more of a thanksgiver—the power of positive thinking and gratitude will surprise you in many ways.
>
> —Dr. Norman Vincent Peale

Gratitude, the true feeling of thankfulness, is crucial to our well-being and key to raising our frequency in order to receive guidance.

John Tierney stated, "Cultivating an attitude of gratitude has been linked to many positive benefits." Gratitude has been linked to better health, sounder sleep, less anxiety and depression, higher long-term satisfaction with life, and kinder behavior toward others, including romantic partners. A new study shows that feeling grateful makes people less likely to turn aggressive.

Upon hearing the results of the study above, who wouldn't want to adapt thankfulness on a regular basis into one's lifestyle? On first blush, you may reason it may seem too difficult or a hassle to practice gratitude. It may seem easier or more fun to gripe and complain. Or you may think to yourself, *"After I deal with my current problems, then I'll begin."* Don't wait. Start today, and become so proficient at being grateful that it becomes second nature. Like attracts like. Demonstrating an attitude of gratitude definitely adds more positivity into your life.

Robert Emmons (2011) reported that listing five things to be thankful for in a gratitude journal, as little as once per week causes noteworthy positive benefits. Emmons related those who use a gratitude journal were "more optimistic, felt happier and feel more refreshed". Initiate your very own journal today!

Individuals who practice a positive, grateful, and lighthearted attitude are vastly different than those who operate from fear and position of scarcity. You have probably witnessed this for yourself. People who sincerely have the mind-set of thankfulness appear to have good things and opportunities come their way inexplicably. These folks appear more youthful, healthier, happier about life, and luckier. On the other hand, the negative-minded person wallows in tough times day after day and never seems to get a break. The vicious cycle of negativity will unfortunately continue since this kind of energy is being thrown into the universe.

A former coworker, "Missy," expressed her miserable feelings to me after her boyfriend had cheated. She cried, "I have nothing now. I am miserable." I was very empathic, yet cautioned Missy not to throw any further negative statements out to the universe since it may attract more. Instead, I instructed her to count her blessings: her two healthy children, owning her own home, and holding a good-paying job. I stated perhaps the universe was demonstrating her boyfriend was not upright and she was being spared even further heartbreak. However, we all understand disappointment and realize it is difficult yet imperative to remain upbeat. Missy's negative mantra continued. Day in and day out, her negativity swirled. Within the week, my coworker's car was hit, her wallet was stolen, and her bank account was compromised. I cautioned her, "Be grateful starting right now. Ask the angels for help, and perform a cleanse immediately!" Missy complied ASAP since she became frightened. Instantly, Missy revealed an optimistic demeanor and encouraging changes started taking place. Today, I hear Missy is happier than ever. She is married to a wonderful man and very grateful that her ex-boyfriend is not a part of her new life.

Beginning today, try an experiment by smiling and using appreciation with true sincerity. Purchase a journal, and log your experiences as Emmons suggested. I am confident you will notice the difference in your life. Even if you feel like you already consider yourself the appreciative type, ramp it up. The benefits will be worthwhile.

Annually, the United States celebrates a holiday on the fourth Thursday of November called Thanksgiving. Americans know Thanksgiving to be the day in 1621 when the Pilgrims and Native Americans celebrated a huge feast together in gratitude. In 1863, Abraham Lincoln announced Thanksgiving as a national holiday in order to praise our heavenly Father. Each year, during Thanksgiving dinner my family practices a tradition. Everyone seated around the dinner table takes a turn and communicates what he or she felt grateful for in the past year. Wouldn't it be a good exercise to proclaim every day as your own personal Thanksgiving Day and take the time each day to reflect, be thankful, and celebrate all of your blessings?

It's all good when you are grateful! You will feel healthier and happier, and your personal and professional relationships become easier. Your mind-set will be that of appreciation, therefore making your channel very clear.

Increase your happiness. Begin today by simply practicing a warm smile with a true heart of thankfulness to God, the angels, the universe, and anyone or anything else you feel is deserving. This new appreciative way of life will produce a shift into your life, such as new opportunities, friends, and feelings. I'm confident fewer whiners and a more fun, lively, and fun-loving crowd will desire to be in your company. As the adage goes, like attracts like, and this proves to be true.

Board the gratitude train today. Your angels will applaud you. Don't forget to appreciate them as well!

> As we express our gratitude, we must never forget that the highest appreciation is not to utter words, but to live by them.
>
> —John F. Kennedy

Chapter 8

Twenty-Five Ways to Remain Positive, Balanced, and Receptive

*A man is but the product of his thoughts;
what he thinks, he becomes.*

—Mahatma Gandhi

∞

It is often an impossible task to maintain a positive attitude 100 percent of the time. On certain days it may seem easier to complain or feel sorry for oneself. Certainly, we all have days in which we feel off balance or not as upbeat. The reasons may be valid. The causes may be due to a bothersome issue, a conflict with a family member, friend, coworker, or simply not feeling well. We are all human, and a certain degree of venting is an acceptable way to unload thoughts and feelings. However, a danger zone is reached when we go beyond a certain point. This can affect our angel communication. Distractions lower our frequency, thus making it more difficult to hear. As we worry and feel tense, our messages will not flow as easily since the mind is cluttered.

It is important to remain calm and content in life. Doing so will counteract the negativity and submerging to low frequency level.

Below I offer to you, in no particular order, twenty-five simple and low- or no-cost recommendations to maintain a blissful life or cheer up when needed. Try a few or all twenty-five. It will produce a happier mind-frame. Plus, your new mood will be infectious to the other people you meet!

1. Embrace Happy Thoughts

Think and manifest victory, accomplishments, love, and fulfillment. Once the mind begins to operate from a positive perspective, the pattern of thoughts will flow easily. With practice, this will become your pattern of thought, and hence happiness will be drawn to you. Living this way will become easy. Subsequently, sending happy feelings into the universe will return them back to you.

2. Practice Affirmations Each Day

First, define your desires. Ask yourself, "What are my dreams, goals, and aspirations?" Once you decide on the most important ones, make a list by placing them into positive statements. Next, believe and act as if they are already true. Place your declarations in the future tense. For example, "I am successful and well respected in my field of study. My children are happy and have loyal, true friends." Since it is always a work in progress, add new wishes to your list as you deem appropriate. Have fun. You are in control. Enlist the aid of your angels for their help, and always remember to show gratitude. Each morning, try logging your affirmations in a planner or journal.

3. Cancel That Thought!

Occasionally, we all think negative thoughts. Usually this undesirable behavior manifests from fear that bubbles to the surface. Cancel it immediately.

One day I was scheduled to present to the board of trustees. Naturally, I was worried and wanted everything to be perfect. My trepidation was that my presentation would be inadequate and sound, for lack of another word, stupid. I noticed my thoughts were drifting and becoming negative. I was thinking, *My material isn't good enough. I will appear senseless and anxious to everyone.* The truth was I was very prepared and knew my material very well. I said to myself, "I'm sabotaging myself!" This thought pattern was certainly not to my benefit or the group's, for that matter. However, there was a way to negate this thinking, and I applied it. As this happens to you, when you doubt yourself and attract negativity, simply state out loud, "Cancel!" The universe will hear it. Another variation you may use is to announce, "Cancel, clear, delete." This is very important since the universe believes anything you tell it. The universe does not realize the difference between the truth and an untruth. It believes what you think or say. Therefore, it is crucial to place positive affirmations out into the cosmos.

In my scenario above, I applied the word *cancel* straightaway. I then implored the angels to be at my side to support me. I received a message to envision the end result I wished from the trustees. I projected the group being very receptive and happy with my clear and factual delivery of information. After the presentation, I received enthusiastic and positive feedback. Needless to say, I was ecstatic! On the drive home, I thanked the angels for their care.

4.   Create a Dream Board

Dream boards are a very creative as well as a personal way to make your dreams come true. Begin by purchasing a simple piece of your favorite colored poster board. On this board, place your hopes and dreams on words and pictures. Paste onto the construction board photos, magazine clippings, stickers, and anything else that may bring to you what you desire. For example, you may desire to have a summer home. Consequently, the board will be filled with your idea of the home you are seeking. If marriage is the dream, place a small picture of your face on the body of a wedding dress or outfit from your favorite bridal magazine. You get the idea. Fill this board with anything you want! Place the board in a spot in which you will be able to gaze upon it often throughout your day or evening. Imagine and believe! These positive thoughts will draw those things to you that you desire! Don't forget to place fanciful pictures of the angels on the board.

Recently, I wanted a particular car. I placed a picture on my board of the exact color and model. One month later I was able to afford it! I love my dream car!

In some cases you don't need be as specific as I was because the Creator may have something better for you than expected. Be patient, and enjoy dreaming and achieving.

5. **Salt Bath**

I'm sure you'll agree that there are certain days that are just exhausting and mentally draining. It is as if everyone else's negativity has stuck to you. A simple solution is to draw a sea salt bath. Please refer to *The Use of Salt* section in Chapter 3.

Always enlist your angels in your endeavors and demonstrate gratitude.

6. **Safeguard Your Chakras**

As described in chapter 3, seven main energy centers exist in various stations of the human body. These centers ensure the body and mind are working together harmoniously. Each chakra is represented by a different color. When an imbalance is experienced, more than likely one or more chakras may be off kilter. This may lead to mental distress or physical illnesses. It is a good idea to cleanse the affected chakras and conduct a full cleanse periodically. It is vital to remain as finely tuned as possible. Of course, communication and intuition will be running at a higher level the cleaner the chakras.

7. **Keep Your Personal Space Uncluttered**

Maintaining a neat and clean living area naturally relieves the mind of clutter. Have you ever observed thinking is easier in an orderly environment? When we experience less confusion, messages will flow more noticeably.

8. **Angel Diary**

The purpose of an angel diary is to record thoughts, desires, and nocturnal dreams. It is a worthwhile avenue to have a chat with your angels regarding your feelings too. They invite you to pour out your heart to them in writing. When doing so, answers will come.

Create a record, and mark the date of each dream or communication. Log the subjects that have been resolved and how. Every so often, revisit your data. It will become apparent how solutions are delivered in a heavenly fashion and in God's timing.

Feel free to use the journal in the back as a starting point. It is a pleasurable exercise that links you to the angelic realm.

9. Release and Surrender Problems to the Creator and His Angels

It is always advisable to surrender problems to God. He and His angelic team will guide you. Have faith, knowing once you relax and give it away to heaven, solutions will arrive. It may not be delivered in your timeframe or in the manner you wish, yet it will be the best outcome for all concerned.

Freedom comes when control is relinquished and trust prevails. As the saying goes, "Let go and let God."

10. Keep Hope in Your Life Every Day

How essential is hope? Apparently so, since the Bible mentions it in excess of 150 times!

One afternoon, I received an angel message regarding hope as I was walking down the street. A troubling circumstance had been on my mind the entire week. I remember feeling temporarily dejected and thinking to myself, *I wonder if there is any hope in this case.* Literally five seconds after I posed the question, my view was directed to a storefront window. In it was a display of framed art. The prominent piece was a silhouette of the Virgin Mary. The words beneath Mary read *HOPE*. It was amazing! It was the perfect sign for me since I had just asked about hope. Feeling relieved, I mentally gave thanks.

Three weeks later, I received good news on the subject. I promised the angels I would share this spirit of optimism with my readers.

It is important to maintain trust in the Supreme.

11. Diffusing Anger

Everyone becomes angered at times. Even the calmest person has moments but may not admit it. It is human nature. However, the level it is demonstrated matters. If you personally have the propensity to reveal your annoyance, remember that you are in control and can manage your emotions. The angels want you to remain happy and positive.

Appeal for help anytime the feeling of irritation begins to bubble. The problem-solving skills of the heavens are much greater than ours. Also, your mood will be elevated just by making the call.

Illustration: "Liz's" daughter was being bullied at school by an older child. The school administration tried to intervene, but it was not working well. Liz wished to make her own stand by taking matters into her own hands. Her plan was to march into school and make a scene in front of the school principal. I cautioned Liz to reconsider and take another approach before pursuing her own. I offered an idea to Liz that included reaching out to the angels. My proposition was to request her daughter's angels speak to the bully's angels. Then, to relate how awful the situation was and to ask them to act as intermediaries and bring a quick resolution.

After Liz glared at me as if I had three heads, she admitted she would try out of desperation. Following personal instruction, Liz gave it a try. Two weeks later, I received a fantastic phone call from Liz. She reported being very relieved. Her daughter had not only received an apology from the bully, but he was also transferring schools. He explained to her that his parents were divorcing and admitted the bullying occurred because he was angry and jealous that she had happily married parents. Liz and I said a prayer to the angels that the boy would find peace in his life. Last we heard, he had, and his parents reconciled.

At some point in our lives, we all experience people who are hurtful or insulting. Another effective course to take when another is hurtful to us is to draft a letter to the angels. Explain the dilemma. After it is written, place this letter in your God box or in another sacred place and wait for results. Don't push; just be patient. Results will come forward as you trust the process.

Moral: Don't ever discount the angels' role in any situation!

12. Positivity or Energized Candles

Candles containing positive energy have been blessed by priests, Reiki masters, or other spiritual officials. These specialized candles offer the light of the Creator and emit blessings and protection for those who burn them.

Infused or religious candles may be purchased from a spiritual shop, a religious store, or online. Different colors represent the different meanings: white, purity and protection, green, health blessings.

Please use caution when burning candles. When finished, please extinguish the candle by using a snuffer. If one is not available, a spoon may be used. It is a much more positive practice to employ a snuffer than to blow out the candle. It is a spiritually better practice and safer as not to spread sparks as well.

13. Motivational Personalities

The purpose of a motivational speaker is to help elevate or positively change a person's mind-set, view, or mental state. They try to propel a change in one's life for the better. Many motivational speakers exist and act as credible and convincing in their oral presentation approach and written word.

I am huge fan of the late Dr. Norman Vincent Peale. He was the author of the famous book *The Power of Positive Thinking*. His thoughts are very inspiring to me. Another personal favorite is Joel Osteen. Joel is a pastor and author who is the host of a very spiritually empowering television show. His program offers wonderful messages. It seems whenever I tune in to his program, he is discussing subject matter that mysteriously answers the questions that are currently on my mind.

I truly believe that many motivational speakers act as agents of God in order to lead us to the answers we need.

14. A Hug

Hugging is a proven way to feel uplifted. By hugging a friend, a spouse, a significant other, a sibling, a child, or even your pet, you are reaping many benefits. As per Urmet Seepter (2013), "The Health Benefits of Hugging," there are three major benefits to hugging:

1. decreases the risk of heart disease,
2. offers stress relief, and
3. is beneficial to your relationship.

A hug can release the hormones serotonin and dopamine and can increase your oxytocin hormone levels, resulting in a happy mood. A hug is also known to lower blood pressure. As we realize, high blood pressure may lead to heart disease.

Virginia Satir, popular noted psychotherapist, suggested, "We need four hugs a day for survival. We need eight hugs a day for maintenance. We need twelve hugs a day for growth."

Give it a try! You can't go wrong with a hug—unless, of course, you try to hug an unwilling participant. This may lead to undue stress and defeat the purpose! Be discriminate.

15. Cheerful Movies and Cartoons

Sounds silly, right? Silly is fun. When seeking lighthearted fun, a comedy or cartoon may be the ticket to lift the spirit. Personally, I always found the Pink Panther and Mr. Bean movies to be mood lifters. After my father died, I watched *Mr. Bean's Holiday*. It was hysterical and brought some relief to me at a sad time.

16. Remember to Laugh and Smile

Studies show laughter is a powerful antidote to stress, pain, and conflict. Laughter brings one's mind into balance, and when the mind is in balance, the physical body will follow. There's nothing like a good laugh. Notice how humor lightens your load; inspires hope; and keeps you grounded, focused, and alert. Force yourself to smile even if you do not wish to do it. It will form a good habit.

17. Keep an Open Mind

Many people claim that opportunities suddenly arise when you approach things in a new way and adopt a fresh way of thinking. Remember—keeping a positive mind-set will attract more positivity into your life.

18. New Experiences

In life, it is important to create different experiences. People generally join a group or begin a hobby as a way to meet like-minded people or as a learning adventure. A few years ago, I had the good fortune of meeting my good friend Hilda during a course. We hit it off immediately and became angel sisters. Although we do not live close to each other, we speak often and share a spiritual connection.

New experiences can be enriching and uplifting.

19. Stop Reliving the Past in Your Mind

If a painful memory exists in your life and is constantly replayed in your head each day—stop! Please do not occupy your precious time in this way. A bright future awaits but will be stalled when a situation is constantly analyzed and reexamined. If the state of affairs can be corrected, do so. If not, purge it from your memory bank. As the negative memory enters your head, replace it with a happy thought immediately. With diligence, this strategy will work.

20. Expressing Gratitude

Take a moment each day to count your blessings and be grateful! The more you do, the more good things will come your way. The law of attraction will be naturally at work.

21. Music

Listening to music is very soothing for the body, soul, and mind. Enjoy music as often as possible. It is known to raise your spiritual frequency while warding off negativity.

22. Prayer

Prayer is a very strong resource and may be said silently, aloud, traditionally, or in your own words. Another form of prayer may be to send an angel to those in need. For instance, as I see an ambulance pass on the highway or a car having trouble at the side of the road, I send angels immediately to assist.

There is a power in prayer, and it returns back to you even stronger.

23. Peace

Peace is priceless. At different points in our lives, we all experience various demands and problems. Possibly sleep is lost, or we do not feel ourselves. At this time, request extra angels into your life to help. You may request peace angels to work with you and lead you back to your former harmonious state. All you have to do is ask. Request peace today!

24. Enjoy a Sunrise or Sunset

Occasionally, make an appointment with yourself to enjoy a sunrise or sunset. It is considered by many to be a very spiritual and calming experience. When we appreciate a sunrise or sunset on a regular basis, a positive shift may be noticed. Relish the quiet time to reflect, appreciate nature, connect and seek guidance, or soul search. It is a time to forget problems and take a break from stress.

A sunrise or sunset is a great reminder of God's infinite beauty.

25. Volunteering

To freely give away one's precious time is a noble thing. Volunteering can be very rewarding and especially fun when you choose a subject that interests you. In this way, you are giving enjoyably while benefiting those in need. If you love what you are doing, it equals success for you and for others.

If volunteering is something your schedule allows, try choosing one that piques your interest. A friend recently offered to volunteer at an animal shelter. She not only loves it but feels she makes a difference. My husband takes joy in feeding the hungry each month at church. I created a visitation program for the sick and homebound. If time allows, consider an agency you would like to help once or twice a month. You will not regret it.

A few nice aspects of volunteering include the enriching feeling associated with it, that the cause is furthered with your help, and that it also seems to provide a mental vacation from one's own pressing matters.

I am confident that by adopting some or all of the ideas above, you will heighten your positive outlook and feel more balanced in life overall. It is much easier to connect with your angels when you are feeling centered and peaceful. God and the angels want us to be happy and to connect with them daily.

~

>   Never give up on a dream just because of the time it will take to accomplish it. The time will pass anyway.
>
>   —Earl Nightingale, American motivational speaker and author

Chapter 9

Setting Objectives and Goals in Order to Communicate with the Angels

> Believe in yourself! Have faith in your abilities!
> Without a humble but reasonable confidence in your
> own powers you cannot be successful or happy.
>
> —Norman Vincent Peale

Objectives and goals are paramount to our lives. Whether we realize it or not, all of us have mental blueprints of the things we wish to attain in our lives. It is no different to set goals and objectives in order to communicate with our angels.

According to Dictionary.com,

> An objective: "Something that one's efforts or actions are intended to attain or accomplish; purpose; goal."

> A goal: "The result or achievement toward which effort is directed; aim; end."

Creating clear objectives and setting goals is done every day by many, such as successful businesspeople, athletes, educators, and even angel believers. In the case of the angel lover, it is a prudent way to begin on your path to gaining insight. No matter the situation, it is vital to an individual's success to create objectives in order to accomplish a desired goal.

The following is a very basic illustration of a goal and objective plan:

The goal is to lose twenty pounds in three months because of an upcoming wedding. The goal is the larger picture.

The objective is to create steps in order to achieve that goal. Therefore, the action plan may consist of a diet plan of fourteen hundred calories coupled with an exercise regime consisting of a thirty-minute aerobics session taking place three days per week. In one month's time, the progress should be accessed and results benchmarked. At that time, if the current weight plateaus, the next objective is to cut down to twelve hundred calories per day and exercise four times per week. This would burn off more calories. In another month, the person will either reach his or her goal or reassess and tweak the objectives to meet the goal.

(Note: This was a very general example, and I would like to stress that I am not a dietician or trained in weight-loss techniques.)

Let's get started with our goals and objectives as it pertains to our angel work. In the previous chapters, I discussed the prep work recommended in order to connect and gain insight from the Divine. This included cleansing, selecting a meditation plan, sticking to a schedule, identifying your strongest clair, and remaining positive and receptive. These are objectives. Our goal is communication from the angelic realm. It is wise to attach a timeline to each objective and measure and benchmark successes. I suggest keeping a journal and have included pages in the back of this book you may use. Often it is helpful to establish short- and long-range goals. This makes it more manageable and less discouraging.

Sample: Angelic Objective and Goal Plan

The goal: To receive clear messages from the Divine.

The objectives:

1. Initially identify your most pronounced clair. Test yourself in everyday life situations by considering the following:

   - Which clair is the strongest?
   - Which clair is my second greatest?
   - Rate the clairs, hearing, seeing, feeling, and knowing, in the order you receive them.
   - Keep a journal. Examine your findings in a week's time.

You will have one clair that is the most forceful, most likely coupled with a secondary clair. My strongest clair is feeling, followed by seeing.

2. Cleanse and stage your specially designated angelic/meditation area.
3. Plan a meditation schedule, and stick to it.
4. Practice forgiveness.
5. Demonstrate gratefulness.
6. Remain positive!

These objectives do not have to be completed all at once. Do not overwhelm yourself. That would prove counterproductive. Allow a reasonable timeframe to achieve your goal.

The absence of a game plan can lead to procrastination. How many times have we said to ourselves, "I will start tomorrow"? However, when that type of thinking occurs, we only slight ourselves.

In short, setting objectives in order to meet a goal is a very practical and worthwhile way to achieve success. As you need assistance, where do you go? Yes, the angels!

Toni Klein, ACP

Any fact facing us is not as important as our attitude toward it, for that determines our success or failure. The way you think about a fact may defeat you before you ever do anything about it. You are overcome by the fact because you think you are.

—Norman Vincent Peale

Chapter 10

THE DOS AND DON'TS WHEN CONNECTING WITH THE ANGELS

Angels encourage us by guiding us onto a path that will lead to happiness and hope.

—Andy Lakey

An important protocol exists in relation to communicating with the angelic realm. Dos and don'ts should be followed.

To begin, it is necessary to provide permission to the angels in order to receive assistance. In a world of free will, this is a perquisite. Consent is vital. At the start of each day, I give the go-ahead to my angels to aid me with all that pertains to my highest good.

As Doreen Virtue (1999) explains in her teachings, the only situation in which your angels will rush to your aid without consent is in a crisis. The angels will only provide you with kind, loving guidance. If something doesn't feel good or happy to you, it is not from the heavens. As Virtue reminds us, messages should be kind. If anything seems scary, it is not from a good source and should be disregarded. Holy angels operate at a high-level frequency and will deliver essential and pleasant messages only unless it involves an immediate warning of danger.

Messages are delivered in many different ways. There is a divine order in life. The answer may not come at the time you expect or in the way you desire. Be aware that if you are not meant to know the answer to your question immediately, it will not be given until you are ready. It's called divine timing. Personally, I took a while to comprehend that since I am the type who wants everything now. However, the angels will not answer unless the timing is right for you. Believe it or not, it is about what is good for you and when. If it is not the appropriate time to hear an answer, it will not be given. Many people expect guidance to be delivered in a timely fashion, loud and clear and with their desired answer. It rarely occurs that way.

The angels may answer softly at times, so listen closely. My experience has been the angels will turn up the volume if you ask in times of worry. When I feel anxious or extremely preoccupied regarding a situation's outcome, they will shout my message since my mind is busy. I am grateful because I would surely miss their words of wisdom.

It is possible to request your messages be delivered in an easily recognizable fashion? Yes. In addition, ask for validation. When you do, validation very often is delivered in three similar yet separate answers. At that point you may rest assured the question has been answered fully by your heavenly team. I often ask for confirmation for my most pressing questions since that is my personality. I need to know. The angels will gladly repeat the answer by showing other signs.

Many years ago, at the time my son, Ian, was to begin attending day care, I was torn between two centers. Naturally, I craved the very best for him. I had one in my mind that was winning but consulted the heavenly kingdom. I sought guidance and received an answer. It was not the answer I expected. I pleaded for evidence since this was a serious matter. Within an hour, I saw a billboard advertising the establishment the angels supported. The next day, I was in a store and heard women speaking about the same day care facility in a positive manner. I received my answer in three different ways. The other company may have been a nice place, but it was not the one for my son's highest good.

Answers are true and consistent. The answer will not change because you want it to be your answer. Frankly, at times you may be disappointed. However, keep the faith. In time, you will clearly see the object of your desire was very wrong for you.

Once an answer is given, God does not change His mind.

Illustration: A friend, "Beth," was interested in a job at an art gallery. It fit perfectly with her schedule and passion for artwork. Although Beth had received three messages indicating this was not in her best interest, she applied anyway. The owner liked her qualifications, and Beth happily accepted the position. She exerted her free will and did not listen to Guidance. After two days on the job, Beth was presented with a much better opportunity that offered more money and travel. Since Beth had committed to the gallery and she had a rapport with the owner, she refused this exciting option. In a few short weeks, the gallery was forced to close. Unfortunately, by that time, the other position had been filled. Beth was crushed when it did not work out on her behalf. However, she admits she was given guidance and chose not to accept it. Today Beth listens and acts on her heavenly advice. Remember—we all make mistakes, and it is never too late to change.

Must Do Recap When Connecting with the Angels
- It is necessary to grant permission to the angels in order receive help. Since humans have free will, they will not interfere.
- Present your question, and pay attention to all signs and messages no matter how trivial. With practice you will fine-tune your skills and notice everything.
- Ask the heavenly beings for another message when clarification or validation is needed. The request is never a bother. Bear in mind, once the answer has been presented, that is the answer. Don't ask over and over because it will not change. The one provided is for your highest good.
- Look for repeated messages. The angels are relating important information to you.

Last year, I saw the word *trust* in three random places. I knew it was related to an issue on my mind. Since I paid attention, everything went well. Yes, trust they are listening and working behind the scenes. It will be on your behalf.

- Do your part. To be given direction is only half the equation. You must do your part as well. Take action. It is up to you bring your plan or desires into fruition.
- I suggest even if you know the meaning of the word provided by the angels, consult a dictionary for all definitions. The word may have another less popular meaning. Check it out. The angels may be expressing themselves in another way than you are accustomed. For example, you may hear the single word *book*. In your mind, it may resonate as reading material. Instead, they may be trying to convey that you will book a trip.
- The angelic team may deliver messages in another language. I was taken aback the first time I received a term in Spanish. Immediately, I consulted the Internet for its translation. Excitedly, I found the interpretation related to my question. Happily I received guidance and learned a new language too!
- After you have enlisted the support of the angels, visualize your desire, and see it as if it has already come to fruition. Picture your goal multiple times per day. Feel in your heart as if it has already materialized.

My good friend Hilda related that her daughter had adopted a little dog named Penny. Shortly after, Penny became very ill. The animal hospital said she had a serious blockage, and delicate surgery was necessary. To aid Penny, Hilda and I called on Archangel Raphael and his healing green light to surround the puppy. Next, we imagined the blockage disappearing. We prayed and visualized often. After the weekend, Penny was given a clean bill of health and sent home. We were so excited and grateful. We thanked Raphael and all the angels for their service.

- Always show respect. Angels are sources directly from the Creator.
- Be sure to enlist other angels in addition to your guardian angel. Many angels are available and are eager to answer your call.

Furthermore, certain angels have specific fortes. You may call upon the angels of love, healing, and success, to name a few. I discuss specific archangels and their specialties in appendix 2.
- Open your mind.
- Believe in yourself.
- Trust.
- Give gratitude.

Don't Recap When Connecting with the Angels
- As you direct your questions to the angels, once is enough. There is no need to echo it to them over and over. They have heard you, so repeating it won't make it come more quickly.
- Don't be bashful. Ask away. Of course, you will be given what you need or is in your best interest. Nevertheless, if you do not even attempt to ask, you will not receive.
- Don't expect guidance to be delivered on your schedule. It will come in its own timing, not yours. To expect an answer on the spot is not reasonable.
- Don't be fearful to ask for an army of angels for help. Your guardian angel will not mind the extra resources.
- Do not have the mind-set that you are asking the angels for too much. Nothing is too big or too small. The Creator knows what you need and don't need. You will be given the correct things.
- Never feel you are unworthy of an answer or help from above.
- Once you receive guidance, don't be fearful to follow it.
- Emotions such as envy, guilt, and fear lower your frequency. Do not succumb to these feelings. It is counterproductive.
- Don't dismiss a message because it is not easily understandable. Angels' messages may not make sense when initially received. Ponder. Explore. It may be a phrase or word not recognizable to you or an old-fashioned phrase not familiar to you.
- Don't be ungrateful or take anything for granted. Every being deserves gratitude, respect, and appreciation.
- Communication with and from Guidance is heavenly! Practice, be diligent, and see the results!

- Don't be impatient. Practice and patience are vital. Everything in life takes time in order to become familiar and see results.
- Don't feel superior. If you think you know better than the Creator and His angels, think again. Do not follow the guidance you are given at your own risk!

Heavenly guidance is a wonderful thing. Cherish it. It is a very special message just for you! You are unique and special! The angels are always willing, but you must do your part too. Stay aware, believe, and take action!

The reason angels can fly is because they take themselves lightly.

—G. K. Chesterton

Example of a smudge stick and fireproof holder.

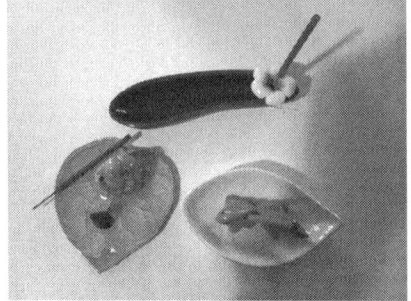

Examples of an incense box, incense towers, and various holders.

Candle snuffers come in many styles.

Select stones, crystals, and oils specifically
geared toward your needs and desires.

You may purchase sea salt from the grocery store, a new-age shop, or actually collect it from the sea. Avoid using regular table salt.

Holy water containers may be purchased in a Catholic shop or be hand crafted from bottles from a local art supply store.

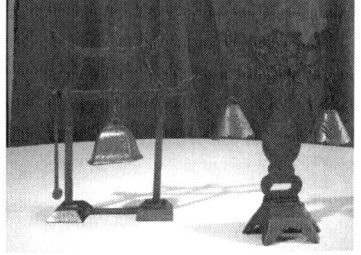

Sanctus bells.

Bells inspired by
the Far East.

Angel bells.
Ring-a-ling-a-ling.
Wave those bells to dispel negativity from your space.
Bells are an individual choice. Select a style to
which you feel a connection. There are no rules.

Antique God Box

Handmade & Souvenir
God Boxes

A God box can be anything you want it to be. It may
be handmade, purchased, or even a souvenir from a
favorite vacation spot. The critical component is that
it holds special meaning and value to the user.

Pendulum and board. The board acts as an assistant for the Q&A session.

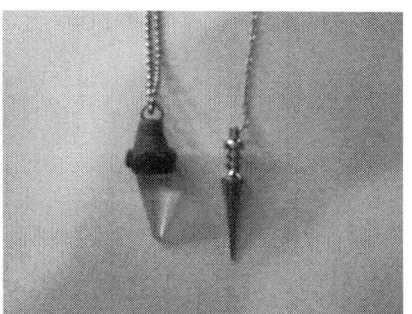

Examples of a handcrafted and industrial made pendulum.

Chanting box and beads. In the Buddhist tradition it is said those who chant "Amituofo" will have an abundance of good fortune, blessings, and protection. Repeating "Amituofo" is a good way to practice meditation.

Designing your very own angel altar is fun! You have creative license. Use unique items special to you such as angel art, essential oils, crystals, and more!

Surround yourself with angel paraphernalia! Such as garden rocks, wooden signs, pretty angel fragrance bottles, or even create angel art such as I did --an angel bling holiday tree.

My beloved church candle holder. I use it before meditating or when concentrating on a special intention.

Our former home was previously located in the center of a triangle of cemeteries. Upon entering a cemetery, you may ask Archangel Michael to protect you against any negative presences that may lurk inside.

My "Spiritual Doggie", Mimi.
(2011-2019)
My precious Mimi lives on forever in my
children's book, *Mimi's Road Trip.*

My awesome angel portrait.
Courtesy of Barbara Thornton.

Chapter 11

Easy Ways to Receive and Recognize Your Guidance

We must be linked up with the Holy Angels: we must form with them one strong family.

—Pope Pius XII

A multitude of avenues exist in which an angel may deliver messages to us. Many people feel it must be very obvious in order to be true guidance. No, not at all. Pay close attention since it may not be in the way you expect!

Listed below are several ways to receive communication:

Meditation

As we have discussed previously, meditation is one of the most valuable tools to enlightenment. Through meditation, the mind becomes clearer while the physical body centers, becomes relaxed, and becomes more receptive.

You may experience some or all of the following:

- Brief or clear vision.
- Recognition the information is true.
- Hearing a word or phrase audibly or inside your head.
- A sensation.

The four clairs will be in gear working for you.

Prayer

Praying is regarded by many as the most powerful method in order to gain insight.

Praying is a valuable practice. Creating your own space special place to pray each day is a nice way to have time for just you. If room allows, try carving out a clean, well-lit, and airy space and decorate your zone with a small altar adorned with candles, crystals, and pictures or statues of angels, saints, or any important religious figure important to you. Ensure its design conforms to your beliefs.

The style in which one prays is an individual choice depending on personal preferance and religious tradition. Some prefer reciting the Catholic rosary while others a Buddhist chant, reading from the Bible or Torah, or engaging in nontraditional, free-form prayer.

Even though it is useful to have a special haven of your very own, prayer may be said in other in other unconventional ways. I frequently pray in the car, silently while standing in a long shopping line, or during my daily walk.

Several friends have shared with me that while praying, they have received signs, thoughts, and ideas. Never underestimate the power of prayer.

Symbolism

Many signs will be transmitted to you mentally through symbolism. Symbolism refers to receiving images in the mind's eye that represent messages. For instance, to see a dove signifies peace, a lion denotes strength, roses exemplify romance, while rings denote a commitment.

Colors also carry meaning. White signifies purity while red represents danger.

Research the images that are presented to you, and relate them to the situations currently in your life. Most likely, you may even develop your own personal image dictionary. It may take a while to compile it. For instance, if an apple flashed through your mind, you may equate this with eating a piece of fruit. However, upon reflection, it may represent a going back to school to further your education or teaching position.

Last year, when I was conducting a reading for a friend, I was presented with an eight ball. In this case, it had nothing to do with a billiard game. Yet your first thought may lead to that conclusion. Rather, the billiard ball, in this scenario, translated to this man experiencing a feeling of being "behind the eight ball" at that period of time in his life. I endorse not jumping to conclusions but rather weighing all the factors in a situation.

With practice, symbolism will become second nature and a valuable resource. In time you will build up your own personal dictionary of images.

Be Still

Messages flow better when the mind is quiet and calm. I notice my communication is heightened while I am on the computer at home. It must feel therapeutic to me since my guidance flows at that time. If my message does not resonate at that moment, I know in the future it will. I quickly make a note in my journal with the date and refer to it later.

On certain occasions, I enlist the assistance of Dictionary.com. Often terms have multiple meanings, and I am interested in knowing which one is meant for me. When I read the choices, I just know. Even though I am familiar with the term, an alternative may offer a better explanation.

I absolutely love when my angels provide a word in a foreign language or an old-fashioned phrase. I know they are not the words I would have spoken. To me, that's true validation the angels are assisting!

Automatic Writing Session

I offer my method of conducting an automatic writing session in the following manner:

- Allow yourself thirty minutes of uninterrupted time for your session.
- Ensure the area is free of all distractions, including the phone, the doorbell, and other individuals in your household. The optimum setting should be serene so that you may clear the mind while holding the intention to communicate.
- Light an unscented, white candle. This will raise the spiritual frequency during the session.
- Recite a brief prayer to Archangel Michael asking him to protect the automatic writing session and to allow only the purest messengers.
- It is best to personalize your own prayer. It can be as simple as saying, "Archangel Michael, please protect my automatic writing session and only allow in messengers and communication that are for my highest good. Thank you."
- Inhale a deep breath in through the nose and then exhale out through the mouth. Repeat two more times. During this process, maintain good thoughts and remain calm.
- Select your method of either a keyboard or traditional pen and paper to conduct the automatic writing.
- Ask a question aloud. Within a few moments, thoughts, visions, or feelings will arrive.
- Write or type whatever is received immediately. Never stop to correct errors, and do not question the communication you will be receiving. Continue writing until you feel the statements have ceased.

Initially, it may seem disappointing or unproductive. Do not get discouraged. In time, you will build confidence and gain experience. Everything in life takes practice.

Overhearing Random Conversations

Have you ever experienced the following situation? While shopping, you overhear a chance conversation between two people nearby. Normally, you mind your own business, but today you couldn't help but listen. Pay attention. Your answer may lie in the stranger's dialogue. This is one valid way the angels speak to you!

Yesterday afternoon, I urgently asked the angels to send me a sign regarding a certain matter. I specifically stated, "Angels, please advise immediately if everything will work out." That night, as I was walking into the store, a customer pushing her shopping cart passed by me. She was on her cell phone instructing the person on the receiving end of the call very loudly, "It will work out. Really it will." I was elated to overhear the statement. I knew the angels had delivered a response to me via the woman in the store. I had used the phrase *work out* in my plea that day. Immediately I thanked the angels and relaxed. Even though it is now difficult to wait, I know it will work out in my favor. The angels often stage a scene for your benefit. It is your part to remain open and aware.

Angel Message Journal
Every single one of us receives a multitude of messages each day. It may consist of a single word that is heard out of the blue. As this happens, it is important to jot these words down for future reference.

Each day I play a word game with my angels. I close my eyes, concentrate, and request a special word particular to my day. Once it has been delivered, I then jot the message down in my journal. If not the same day, later this word or phrase will make sense and have bearing in my life. Some words may act as reminders, however. Today, my word was *blessings*. I was thankful immediately. Sometimes in life when we worry about our daily details, we tend to forget to take the time to take stock of our blessings and give thanks.

One morning, I heard the single word *daffodil*. I was surprised since it is not a flower I would normally purchase or a word I ordinarily use. I took note of daffodil in my journal, dated it, and then dismissed the word from my mind. Two weeks later, daffodils were placed on the altar for Palm Sunday. One of the parishioners was not able to attend that day. She left word to give the daffodil she had purchased to me after the service ended. Instantly, I remembered my angel word *daffodil*. They had informed me in advance about these pretty flowers I was to enjoy as well as highlighting the generosity of others. This story illustrates not all messages will be life altering. Sometimes it is just a reminder the angels are constantly there and love to communicate with us.

Dreams

Dreams are wonderful way to receive messages from the angelic realm. Immediately before drifting off to sleep, present your concern or question clearly and plainly. My mother and brother endorse this practice since they have had much success. They attest the answer will be presented within one week or less from the date of the inquiry.

Upon awakening, log all memories of the dream and feelings you are experiencing. I suggest immediately since the memory will vanish as the day unfolds. It is very easy to forget what messages delivered to us. Keep the angel diary and pen always accessible next your bedside.

Evaluate your documentation at the end of each week. You may even find it beneficial to purchase a dream dictionary as well. There are many choices available.

I endorse placing a clear crystal on the bedside table since the clear crystal is said to enhance the clarity of one's dreams.

Sweet dreams!

Guidance Assistance Tools

Certain tools may be employed in an effort to receive guidance more quickly and easily. I have listed for you below the ones I have found work very well:

Authentic Crystals and Stones

A variety crystals or angel stones are known to raise your vibration and enhance your connectivity to the angelic realm. Do not purchase man-made versions since they do not possess the power of nature.

There are many ways to utilize crystals or stones, such as placing them on an angel altar, wearing them as jewelry, carrying them on the body in a pouch, or meditating with them in the palm of your hand.

Below is a partial list that will bring you closer to the angels and heighten your power:

- amethyst
- angelite
- celestine
- moldavite
- orange elestial
- petalite
- rainbow fluorite
- selenite
- sodalite

For more information, visit a New Age store or visit a specialty shop online. The staff should be very knowledgeable and answer your questions regarding a particular need or stone quest. There are various stones that assist with different ventures.

Once the stone or crystal has been handpicked, ensure the proper steps are taken to cleanse it. Many hands have touched the stones in the store so it is important for you to properly cleanse it prior to use. Wash away any residual negativity by rinsing the stone or crystal briefly with a mixture of sea salt and water. Do not soak the crystals for long periods of time since the sea salt may dissolve them. Another option is placing it in direct sunlight for a day. Stones and crystals may be charged in the moonlight on the windowsill overnight. This is not a cleansing solution but rather adds energy to your crystal.

Do not allow anyone else to handle your crystals once they are cleansed. You were the only person who should touch and energize your personally selected stones. If this occurs, recleanse them immediately.

Angel Cards

Angel oracle cards may act as another useful tool to in order to communicate with our heavenly team. A card deck includes approximately forty cards, each depicting an illustration with the meaning of the card below it.

Oracle cards may be used for daily guidance or advice. The reader's question is answered by drawing one card at a time or by laying out several cards in a spread. You may personally conduct your own reading or have an experienced reader conduct a formal reading.

A variety of decks are available for sale on many topics of interest, such as healing or romance.

Oracle cards may be purchased online, in a bookstore, or in a New Age shop. Oracle card apps are even available to download on the smartphone. Personally I love the phone apps and use them each day to draw my daily card.

Pendulums

Pendulums are employed to answer a yes-or-no question only. The pendulum does not provide detailed answers. Therefore, the question cannot be open ended. A simple question could be, "Will I receive my promotion?" The question cannot be phrased, "What salary will I receive for my promotion?"

Prior to use, your pendulum needs to be instructed as to which direction is yes and which direction is no. I always choose a right swing meaning yes and the opposite as no.

The pendulum can be homemade or purchased from a specialty shop or craft fair. A handcrafted pendulum may be as simple as threading a needle with white thread. Typically pendulums are made with crystals, metal, or wood and attached to a chain or cord.

Runes

As per encyclopedia.com, a *rune* is an ancient alphabet written on rocks and belongs to the Germanic group. Runes can be traced as far back as the third century.

The intent of the runes is not to forecast a future event but rather provide present-day guidance. Its premise is not to project but offer a path choice for those who seek answers.

The questions posed must be pointed rather than general. A question may be phrased in the following fashion: "Please advise how I may attain a quick and happy resolution concerning (mention specific issue now)." Do not phrase the question too generally. For example, "What shall I do?"

Bear in mind, the job of the runes is not to be a prophecy of events to come. It is simply a communication technique to cast light on present situations.

Naturally, the clairs will come into play while utilizing runes. Focus.

Today, simulated runes are available to the user online, at spiritual fairs, or in kits with instructions available in bookstores.

Overall, I recommend using your judgment and discretion with all tools that augment your own gift of knowing, seeing, feeling, and hearing. I have known those who prefer use to certain tools to augment their spiritual gifts only in the beginning stages until their confidence has been raised. Others only use the tools occasionally.

Everyone has individual tastes. Do what brings you happiness and produces the best results.

Remember—we all have free will. An answer to a question you have been given today may change tomorrow based on your actions and choices. Nothing is written in stone or is considered permanent.

Once you recognize and experience true guidance, your spiritual antenna will raise, therefore making you more aware and turned in. Messages will appear in various ways and when least expected, usually when you are very relaxed. Your job is to make these connections and know the communication you are seeking is real.

Illustration: Stan is a single man and currently is not in a relationship. Recently, he asked the angels of love and romance to direct him to his true love. Shortly after his petition, Stan began to hear the same love song on the radio each day. It was always playing as he passed the church near his neighborhood. Later that week, Stan observed a billboard in front of the church which read, "Singles dance Friday night."

Toni Klein, ACP

Since Stan had petitioned the angels, two choices of action were laid before him. One: Stan could figure there wasn't a correlation and ignore the signs by figuring it was random information. Two: Stan has been confident the heavens would hear his plea and has been watching closely for signs. Therefore, Stan decides to attend the singles function at the church since he is being drawn there. Let's now fast forward in time to the present day. Stan has been happily married to the love of his life. Three years ago Stan asked, listened, took action, and is grateful. Way to go Stan! See how this works?

Our angels are here to help us every day. They are concerned with our well-being and the goals we have set for ourselves on this earth. At times when we feel they are not with us or hearing us or have forgotten us, that certainly is not the case. As we are pondering, "Where did they go?" they are behind the scenes working on our hopes and dreams when in our best interests.

Pay attention to your daily messages. You'll be happy you did!

As I was writing this chapter I received a message for you from the angels. They related, "Do not miss the seemingly little things, for it could be one of your greatest messages!"

～

> Pay attention to your dreams—God's angels often
> speak directly to our hearts we are asleep.
>
> —Eileen Elias Freeman

Chapter 12
LIVING YOUR LIFE WITH THE ANGELS

Make yourself familiar with the angels and behold them frequently in spirit; for without being seen, they are present with you.

—St. Francis De Sales

Life with the angels is a glorious adventure. They are your friends, protectors, confidants, and much more! Remember to treat them this way. Just as you automatically trust a bridge to carry you safely across the waters or a chair to support you as you sit, trust that these heavenly beings are there for you.

As your angel awareness increases and you begin to incorporate them into your daily existence, a noticeable shift will occur. Your days will seemingly become easier, lighter, and brighter and your messages clearer.

Converse often, and share your day, desires, hopes, and dreams with your fanciful friends. These beings are there for you and happy to be included!

Living a life close to the angels can offer the following:

Toni Klein, ACP

- A feeling of security.
- A feeling of peace and well-being.
- Guidance filled with love and peace.
- An existence with less stress.
- Protection for you and loved ones.

Kudos to you! You have entered a transformational period. Enjoy the journey!

∼

For every soul, there is a guardian watching it.

—The Koran

Epilogue

Congratulations! There's a spiritual reason you purchased *Passport to Heaven's Angelic Messages*. A message to connect with guidance was sent on your behalf. Go forward and put your desire to connect with the heavens into action. They are waiting.

In order to be an effective communicator and receiver of guidance, be sure to employ all the steps provided. Maximize your power of connecting by doing the following:

- Identifying your predominant clair.
- Cleansing.
- Staging.
- Developing a meditation plan and enforcing it.
- Practicing forgiveness.
- Expressing sincere gratitude.
- Remaining positive.
- Practicing the dos and don'ts of communicating with the angels.
- Living an enhanced life with a solid connection to the Creator.

As I was writing this epilogue, I received an important angelic message for everyone:

> Enjoy life. Don't experience feelings of guilt regarding any mistakes you may have made in the past. If you have learned from the experience and do not repeat the behavior, let it go. Move forward. Concentrate on living a happy and productive life. Be kind to yourself and others. Focus on positivity and serving in some way.

> Your frequency will be raised. Be elated, live life to the fullest, and listen for our guidance. We are always there for you.

If you care to share feedback or an angel experience, feel free to email me: toniklein@ymail.com

Please visit: https://www.tonikleinauthor.com

https://www.facebook.com/Tonikleinauthor/

Thank you for choosing *Passport to Heaven's Angelic Messages.*

I wish you much success, happiness, and beautiful messages!

Peace and light,

Toni

Appendix 1
ANGEL EXPERIENCES

All God's angels come to us disguised.

—James Russell Lowell

~

The following beautiful angel stories have been related to me in order to share with you, my angelic readers. I hope you feel a part of these true real-life testimonials. It is truly amazing how the angels help us in our lives each and every day.

Enjoy!

* * *

In 1990, I suddenly became ill. I had difficulty breathing and was tired all the time. I went to see the doctor, and after running numerous tests, they found that I had an obstruction in my lung and I needed to have surgery. During this time, I became very scared and nervous.

One evening I started to pray. As I was praying, I saw the most beautiful angel standing beside me. I knew he was the angel of healing. In an instant, all the fear and nervousness I was experiencing was taken from me. I was overwhelmed with a warm, peaceful energy going through my entire body. In that moment, I knew I didn't have to be afraid, that everything would turn out okay. I had the surgery, and to the doctor's amazement, I recovered very quickly.

Hilda

* * *

Years ago (before cell phones were invented), my husband, Dave, and I were on our way to New Hampshire. While Dave was driving through Springfield, Massachusetts, we encountered a flat tire. We panicked since it was late and snowing very hard. Dave and I were wondering how we were going to find a place to use the phone to call for assistance when all of a sudden a very kind-looking guy with bright blue eyes jumped out of his van to help. Quicker than you could believe, the flat was substituted for the spare. Of course, this enabled us to drive to the nearest tire store the next day! Dave was so grateful, and he was trying to insist that the young man take some money for his kindness. The guy simply said, "No, God bless you both." We looked back and he was gone! Honestly, we both said to each other, "That must have been an angel." We have talked many times about it since. Our dog, Topper, was in the backseat and never even barked!

Joan

* * *

Years ago, I was considering buying an old cast-iron fireplace from a local antique shop. It was from the late 1800s, and I was in love with it. Unfortunately, I was broke and they only accepted cash. I thought if I called my credit card company, I could get a cash advance to buy it. I owed a lot on my card, and it was a true extravagance. I made the call and explained what I needed. I encountered a very lovely woman who said to me, "Don't do it! It's a financial gas chamber." (She was referring to me taking the cash advance.) I was amazed she wished to dissuade me since she was employed by the credit card company, whose business was to make money. I thought to myself, *She is right! Forget this.* To this day, I believe she was an angel trying to help me with my finances. Plus, my husband surprised me with the fireplace later on! An angel sits on top of it today!

Jamie

* * *

I was dating a beautiful woman who I considered an angel. She was visiting me one evening and left the room for a brief moment. After she stepped away, the living room filled with a bright light, and I saw a mystical figure. It said to me, "I am not here for you. I am here for her. It is your job to look after her. We will help you, but she needs you too." With that, the figure was gone. I was shocked and couldn't move. I remember I had a few magnets in the room, which I had bought on vacation. They all became demagnetized. I believe in angels. I was so amazed and happy one appeared and spoke to me!

Hank

* * *

I was seeing a new guy who I really wanted to marry. Often we would sit together by the river and watch the boats go by. One weekend, Jake was away, so I went back to sit by the river to feel close to him. It was crowded that day, and many people were there. I didn't realize it, but I had closed my eyes and started to chant silently, "I want him. I want him." Suddenly, a masculine voice said loudly to me, "He's yours!" I opened my eyes to see who was talking to me, and no one was there. I sat there dumbfounded. A few minutes later, a man singing a spiritual hymn walked by me and smiled. An angel spoke to me and assured me it was going to work out with us! My guy and I will be married five years this fall.

Jamie

* * *

I had worked many years for the same company, and it had downsized a few times. Initially, I had a very good position with the company for over fifteen years. However, during one of the downsizing transitions, I was demoted to a lower position. After what I had been doing, it was an awful demotion. It seemed as if the president of the company enjoyed seeing my job change and on top of that, was out to get me. Many games were played, and unfairness occurred. The hours were still civilized and I needed the money, so I stuck with it.

Each Monday, the managers were required to attend a weekly meeting. I was sitting at the table when a voice said to me, "He will get you one more time. It will be a blow to you." I understood what I heard and mentally prepared myself. It meant the president would demote me again and into an even worse spot. Two weeks later, I was called in and given almost the worst management job there. Plus, the hours were horrible and it conflicted with the time I could spend with my family. Indeed, it was a big blow to me. But I needed the money so I had to stay, but I decided to look for another place of employment.

I prayed every day, sometimes all day, to be able to find a new, wonderful job with good hours for me and my family. I was suffering since everything was getting worse and I was miserable. One day, while walking into the job, I heard, "You will get out right before they get you." I lived by this message and had faith I would get out of there soon and on my own terms. I continued to pray, yet nothing happened. Then, one day a friend called to tell me to hurry and apply for a job in her institution. I did, but the process was a long one. I continued to pray and every day repeated the angel's message to myself. I knew I would be saved from that horrible job.

One happy summer day, I got the call I was waiting for. The new job with great hours and pay was mine. I was able to be with my family again. Before I could give notice that day, I was called into the president's office. He informed me I was being transferred to an even worse position. I didn't think a worse one was possible. I laughed at him and stated I was giving my notice because I was leaving for an ideal position with great hours and pay! His face fell. Overall, it was a wonderful angelic experience. To this day, I am still very grateful for my angelic help and my messages. Those messages got me through a very difficult time in my life. I believed what I was told. The messages were important. The angels told me I would get out before they got me. I did. Without God and His angels, I don't know what would have happened to me. To this day, I'm still grateful and thank God and my angels every day!

Anthony

These things I warmly wish for you. Someone to love, some work to do, A bit o' sun, a bit o' cheer, And a guardian angel always near.

—Irish blessings

Appendix 2
THE HIERARCHY OF ANGELS

> For He will give His angels charge of you, to guard you in all your ways. On their hands they will bear you up, lest you dash your foot against a stone. (Psalm 91:11–12)

According to various sources, nine choirs of angels exist. They are divided into three triads. The top three belong to the highest-ranking order; the middle level is the second choir, and the third and last choir of angels is the lowest-ranking order.

Seraphim	First choir of angels
Cherubim	
Thrones	
Dominions	Second choir of angels
Virtues	
Powers	
Principalities	Third choir of angels
Archangels	
Angels	

1. Seraphim
- Seraphim were mentioned in the Old Testament and are considered to be the highest-ranked order of angels.
- Seraphim are stationed by God's throne to serve Him.
- Seraphim surround the throne of God and continuously chant, "Holy, Holy, Holy" in a very melodic fashion.
- Seraphim means "ardor."
- They radiate bright light.
- They are coined "fiery serpents" in appearance since they emanate love and light.

2. Cherubim
- Cherubim are located in the first tier directly below the seraphim and possess the knowledge of God.
- Cherubim symbolize power and mobility since they are depicted as charioteers.
- They are known as loving beings.
- They are considered the bridge between the spiritual and material realms.
- They are described in lore as having a "sphinxlike" appearance.

3. Thrones
- Thrones are the last group in the first choir of angels and denote humility, peace, and submission.
- The thrones are needed by the lower-ranking angels in order to be admitted into God's direct realm.
- Thrones have been characterized as having many glowing eyes and take the form of a wheel-like shape.

4. Dominions
- Dominions are the first set of angels in the second choir and are known as the angels of leadership.
- Dominions ensure the commands of God are carried out.
- They are the go-betweens for the higher and lower choirs of angels.
- They regulate duties of the lower-ranking angels.
- They rarely reveal themselves to humans.

5. Virtues
- Virtues are fifth in the placement line and are referred to as the spirits of motion or "shining ones."
- These angels exercise authority over nature: the elements, moon, stars, planet, and seasons.
- Virtues guard the planet.
- Virtues are also linked to courage and miracles.
- These angels are fifth in the line of placement.

6. Powers
- Powers are the sixth in line of the nine orders of angels. They are referred to as the warrior angels or guards.
- They ensure souls reach heaven safely.
- They defend humans and creation against evil spirits.
- Therefore, these beings are named as the favorites of humankind.

7. Principalities
- Principalities are located at the top of the final choir of angels. The duty of the principalities is to watch over mortals. They protect the world's towns, cities, and nations.
- They carry out heavenly acts concerning their area of jurisdiction.
- They manage the duties for the angel choir.

8. Archangels
- Archangels are second-to-last rank in the overall hierarchy. They are referred to as the chief angels or special angels.
- These angels are the most frequently mentioned in the NIV Bible.
- Archangels act as messengers to humans.
- They act as the guardians over the church for bishops, cardinals, and various rulers.
- They are mentioned in Judaism, Christianity, and Islam.
- Archangels oversee the guardian angels and humans.
- One popular example of an archangel is Archangel Michael, the protector.

9. Angels
- Angels are the last in the order. These celestial beings are the closest to earth and include the guardian angels.
- Angels are the closest to earth and humans.
- Angels deliver the prayers of the earthly humans to God as well as His answers back to the people.
- They have the power to invoke the angels of any other level at any time.
- Angels are known to be caring and patient.
- Angels are the last level of the spectrum.

And I saw another angel flying through the sky, carrying the eternal Good News to proclaim to the people who belong to this world— to every nation, tribe, language, and people. (Revelation 14:6)

Appendix 3
WHO ARE THE ARCHANGELS AND ANGELS?

Angel of God, my guardian dear to whom God's love commits me here; Ever this day be at my side, to light and guard, to rule and guide.

—Old English Prayer

Below is a list of the seven archangels who are widely discussed throughout the world of angels. The Roman Catholic Church recognizes the first three archangels: Michael, Gabriel, and Raphael. The Old Testament spoke of Michael and Raphael only. It wasn't until the New Testament that more archangels were added. Notice the *el* in the word *angel*. El means, "In God."

Listed below are seven well-known archangels:

Michael
Gabriel
Raphael
Uriel
Chamuel
Jophiel
Raguel

1. Michael
- Known as "He is who is like God," Michael has been said to be the greatest of all the angels. He is in charge of the order of all angels and the leader of the archangels. Michael is the known protector.
- Archangel Michael also assists the light workers of the world. You may feel heat when Archangel Michael is near.
- Michael will assist you with the following when asked:
    - He escorts away lower energy and rids negativity.
    - He offers encouragement and strength.
    - He encourages and motivates.
    - Prior to bedtime, you may request Michael to enter into your dreams in order to release any fears.
    - Another specialty of Michael's is to assist you with any electrical or mechanical issues.
2. Gabriel
- Referred to as the messenger angel or messenger of God, Gabriel means "strength of God."
- In the Old Testament, Gabriel appeared to Mary to inform her about Jesus's impending birth.
- Gabriel also is known to assist with the following:
    - If you are interested in writing or publication, Gabriel is your angel! He also guides those who are in or are interested in television or radio careers.
    - Connects you to your own personal power and spiritual gifts.
    - Assists mothers with the adoption or birthing process.
    - Inspires and motivates.
    - Guides those in the fields of communication.
3. Raphael
- In the Hebrew language, "Rapha" means healer or doctor. Raphael is known as, "He who heals."
- Raphael may assist you in the following ways: physically, mentally, and spiritually in regard to humans and animals. Raphael is

associated with green light. Therefore, if you experience flashes of green light, he is making his presence known to you.
- He can guide you to a healthier life.
- He transforms thoughts and fears to a healthier way of thinking.

4. Uriel
- Uriel is located at the head of the third choir of angels. He has been described as, "God is light," "Fire of God," "Sun of God," and "Flame of God."
- This archangel offers assistance to us in the following areas:
    - Creativity and mental thought processes.
    - Heightening our claircognizance (knowingness) ability.
    - Provides warning of danger to us.
    - Provides light to our lives when needed.

5. Chamuel
- Chamuel is known as, "He who is God." This archangel is the powerful leader in the powers hierarchy of angels.
- Below are the attributes of Chamuel:
    - Chamuel helps you find your or life's path or mission.
    - He protects the world.
    - He aids with employment and career issues.
    - He assists with locating your soul mate.
    - He repairs situations with partner relationships in love or business.

6. Jophiel
- Jophiel means, "Beauty of God."
- Jophiel offers assistance to you in the following areas when invoked:
    - Unclutters the mind of negative thinking.
    - Clears away negative energy.
    - Offers peace and positivity.
    - Specialty is helping those in the artistic careers.
    - Wishes us to appreciate Mother Nature and think thankful thoughts.

7. Raguel
- Raguel is known as the "friend of God."
- Raguel will help us when called with the following:
  - To increase our clairsentience ability ("gut feelings").
  - To guide us to loving people and situations.
  - To give harmony in relationships.
  - Provides solutions to problems; resolves conflicts.
  - Assists in the defense of those being mistreated or unfairly.

Archangels are omnipresent, which means they may be with you and others at the same time. Never be shy when calling on them, and don't be stressed that your request isn't large enough for their attention. Remember—since humans have free will, an angel will never interfere with a person's life unless asked (except in emergency situations).

Guardian Angels

Everyone has at least one guardian angel at his or her side at all times. I believe you have probably been familiar with them since childhood. Earlier, I listed the Old English Prayer, "Angel of God, my guardian dear to whom God's love commits me here; Ever this day be at my side, to light and guard, to rule and guide."

Yes, we all have a guardian angel, which is certainly a comforting thought. Your angel is unique to you and is your very own loving protector. It has been with you since birth and shall remain until you have safely crossed over to the other side.

Communicate constantly with your angel and share your life. Your angel has an investment in you and wants to be a part of everything! Your guardian angel is assigned to you and no one else. Therefore, your angel won't fly off to assist another person or find anyone else's problems bigger than your own.

Often, the term *spirit guide* is interchanged with *guardian angel*. Even though both guide and protect us, there are differences. An angel is light and energy from the Creator and has never lived a life in human form.

Also, an angel's vibration and energy are much higher than that of a guide. On the other hand, your spirit guide was a human being who lived on earth and most likely is generations older than you are. For example, the presence of a great-grandmother could be a spirit guide to a baby born today. Differences do exist between the terms *angels* and *guides*. However, the presence of the spirit guide is not to be devalued in any sense. They love us and are an important part of our lives as well.

Angels

The angels are God's gifts to us. Angels are not to be worshiped. That is reserved for God.

Angels are sent to us by God and will answer our calls when we need them. There is an abundance of unassigned angels waiting for our call. They are overjoyed to help. No request is too monstrous or too silly. These angels may help us in a variety of ways with anything from finding the perfect outfit for a party to a much more serious situation.

In cases in which God feels we are not ready or should not be provided with the answer to a particular question at that particular moment we ask, our request may not be answered. It is all about divine timing and what is for your highest good. God knows you better than anyone else does. Your prayer for assistance may be delayed on purpose. Or the angels may plan to deliver something to you that is much, much better! Remember the old saying "Be careful what you wish for"? This is true. The angels and the Creator have your back.

Please remember that everyone has free will and must give permission to the angels in order to receive assistance unless it is a crisis situation.

And one last reminder—angel etiquette is necessary! Thank the Creator and His angelic team while keeping gratitude in your heart and life!

Toni Klein, ACP

When I was a child I thought I saw an angel. It had wings and kinda looked like my sister. I opened the door so some light could come into the room, and it sort of faded away. My mother said it was probably my Guardian Angel.

—Denzel Washington

Appendix 4
ARCHANGEL MODALITIES

I saw the angel in the marble and carved it until I set it free.

—Michelangelo

The following is a short list of the strengths the archangels possess. Please feel free to call on them and their area of specialty when you need help in one or more of the areas.

Archangel Ariel: Protects animals

Archangel Azrael: Crosses souls into heaven, grief assistance

Archangel Chamuel: Harmony, relationships, building friendships, conflict resolution, romance

Archangel Gabriel: Communication skills, clear decision making, child rearing

Archangel Jophiel: Beauty

Archangel Metatron: Patron angel of small children, aids with childhood issues

Archangel Michael: Strength, courage, protection

Toni Klein, ACP

Archangel Phanuel: Repentance, hope

Archangel Raphael: Healing

Archangel Raquel: Resolves conflicts, helps harmonize personal or business relationships

Archangel Raziel: Clears blockages so guidance may be received

Archangel Sandalphon: Patron angel of music; carries prayers to God in heaven

Archangel Uriel: Patron angel of literature, wisdom, creativity, knowledge; helps students with test taking

Where saints and angels dwell above, all hearts are knit in holy love.

—Henry Williams Baker

REFERENCES

Alden, Ginger. 2014. *Elvis and Ginger.* New York: The Berkley Publishing Group.

Catalfo, Phil. 2015. Chakras 101 http://www.naturalhealthmag.com/mind-body/chakras-101.

CBS News. 2011. http://cbsnews.com.

Duin, Julia. 2008. http://www.washingtontimes.com/news/2008/sep/19/half-of-americans-believe-in-angels/?page=all.

Emmons, Robert. 2010. "Why Gratitude is Good." http://greatergood.berkeley.edu/article/item/why_gratitude_is_good/.

Encyclopedia.com http://www.encyclopedia.com.

Fairchild, Mary. 2011. "What Does the Bible Say About Angels?" http://christianity.about.com/od/whatdoesthebiblesay/a/angelsbible.htm.

O'Brien, Melissa. 2011. "What are the Cognitive Benefits of Meditation?" http://www.quora.com/What-are-the-cognitive-benefits-of-meditation.

Peale, Vincent. 1952. *The Power of Positive Thinking.* New York: Prentice Hall.

Satir, Virginia. http://mobile.brainyquote.com/.

Seepter, Urmet. 2012. "The Health Benefits of Hugging." http://goodrelaxation.com/2012/03/the-health-benefits-of-hugging/.

Tierney, John. 2011. "A Serving of Gratitude May Save the Day." http://www.nytimes.com/2011/11/22/science/a-serving-of-gratitude-brings-healthy-dividends.html

Virtue, Doreen. 1999. *Healing with the Angels. Carlsbad*, CA: Hay House Publishing.

Yoga Journal. YJ. 2012. http://www.yogajournal.com/uncategorized/new-study-finds-20-million-yogis-u-s/.

Journal

Journal

Journal

Journal

Journal

Printed in Great Britain
by Amazon